# POLLS AND THE MEDIA IN CANADIAN ELECTIONS

~

*This is Volume 16 in a series of studies
commissioned as part of the research program
of the Royal Commission on Electoral Reform
and Party Financing*

# POLLS AND THE MEDIA IN CANADIAN ELECTIONS
## TAKING THE PULSE

~

Guy Lachapelle

Volume 16 of the Research Studies

ROYAL COMMISSION ON ELECTORAL REFORM
AND PARTY FINANCING
AND CANADA COMMUNICATION GROUP –
PUBLISHING, SUPPLY AND SERVICES CANADA

DUNDURN PRESS
TORONTO AND OXFORD

© Minister of Supply and Services Canada, 1991
Printed and bound in Canada
ISBN 1-55002-112-5
ISSN 1188-2743
Catalogue No. Z1-1989/2-41-16E

Published by Dundurn Press Limited in cooperation with the Royal
Commission on Electoral Reform and Party Financing and Canada
Communication Group – Publishing, Supply and Services Canada.

**Canadian Cataloguing in Publication Data**

Lachapelle, Guy, 1955–
    Polls and the media in Canadian elections

(Research studies ; 16)
Issued also in French under title: Les sondages et les médias lors des
    élections au Canada.
ISBN 1-55002-112-5

    1. Public opinion polls. 2. Public opinion – Canada. 3. Mass media –
Political aspects – Canada. 4. Electioneering – Canada. 5. Elections –
Canada. I. Canada. Royal Commission on Electoral Reform and Party
Financing. II. Title. III. Series: Research studies (Canada. Royal Commission
on Electoral Reform and Party Financing) ; 16.

JL193.L25 1991      324.7'3'0971      C91-090528-2

$19.95

Dundurn Press Limited              Dundurn Distribution
2181 Queen Street East             73 Lime Walk
Suite 301                          Headington
Toronto, Canada                    Oxford, England
M4E 1E5                            OX3 7AD

# CONTENTS

# FIGURES

# TABLES

# FOREWORD

THE ROYAL COMMISSION on Electoral Reform and Party Financing was established in November 1989. Our mandate was to inquire into and report on the appropriate principles and process that should govern the election of members of the House of Commons and the financing of political parties and candidates' campaigns. To conduct such a comprehensive examination of Canada's electoral system, we held extensive public consultations and developed a research program designed to ensure that our recommendations would be guided by an independent foundation of empirical inquiry and analysis.

The Commission's in-depth review of the electoral system was the first of its kind in Canada's history of electoral democracy. It was dictated largely by the major constitutional, social and technological changes of the past several decades, which have transformed Canadian society, and their concomitant influence on Canadians' expectations of the political process itself. In particular, the adoption in 1982 of the *Canadian Charter of Rights and Freedoms* has heightened Canadians' awareness of their democratic and political rights and of the way they are served by the electoral system.

The importance of electoral reform cannot be overemphasized. As the Commission's work proceeded, Canadians became increasingly preoccupied with constitutional issues that have the potential to change the nature of Confederation. No matter what their beliefs or political allegiances in this continuing debate, Canadians agree that constitutional change must be achieved in the context of fair and democratic processes. We cannot complacently assume that our current electoral process will always meet this standard or that it leaves no room for improvement. Parliament and the national government must be seen as legitimate; electoral reform can both enhance the stature of national political institutions and reinforce their ability to define the future of our country in ways that command Canadians' respect and confidence and promote the national interest.

In carrying out our mandate, we remained mindful of the importance of protecting our democratic heritage, while at the same time balancing it against the emerging values that are injecting a new dynamic into the electoral system. If our system is to reflect the realities of Canadian political life, then reform requires more than mere tinkering with electoral laws and practices.

Our broad mandate challenged us to explore a full range of options. We commissioned more than 100 research studies, to be published in a 23-volume collection. In the belief that our electoral laws must measure up to the very best contemporary practice, we examined election-related laws and processes in all of our provinces and territories and studied comparable legislation and processes in established democracies around the world. This unprecedented array of empirical study and expert opinion made a vital contribution to our deliberations. We made every effort to ensure that the research was both intellectually rigorous and of practical value. All studies were subjected to peer review, and many of the authors discussed their preliminary findings with members of the political and academic communities at national symposiums on major aspects of the electoral system.

The Commission placed the research program under the able and inspired direction of Dr. Peter Aucoin, Professor of Political Science and Public Administration at Dalhousie University. We are confident that the efforts of Dr. Aucoin, together with those of the research coordinators and scholars whose work appears in this and other volumes, will continue to be of value to historians, political scientists, parliamentarians and policy makers, as well as to thoughtful Canadians and the international community.

Along with the other Commissioners, I extend my sincere gratitude to the entire Commission staff for their dedication and commitment. I also wish to thank the many people who participated in our symposiums for their valuable contributions, as well as the members of the research and practitioners' advisory groups whose counsel significantly aided our undertaking.

Pierre Lortie
Chairman

# INTRODUCTION

THE ROYAL COMMISSION'S research program constituted a comprehensive and detailed examination of the Canadian electoral process. The scope of the research, undertaken to assist Commissioners in their deliberations, was dictated by the broad mandate given to the Commission.

The objective of the research program was to provide Commissioners with a full account of the factors that have shaped our electoral democracy. This dictated, first and foremost, a focus on federal electoral law, but our inquiries also extended to the Canadian constitution, including the institutions of parliamentary government, the practices of political parties, the mass media and nonpartisan political organizations, as well as the decision-making role of the courts with respect to the constitutional rights of citizens. Throughout, our research sought to introduce a historical perspective in order to place the contemporary experience within the Canadian political tradition.

We recognized that neither our consideration of the factors shaping Canadian electoral democracy nor our assessment of reform proposals would be as complete as necessary if we failed to examine the experiences of Canadian provinces and territories and of other democracies. Our research program thus emphasized comparative dimensions in relation to the major subjects of inquiry.

Our research program involved, in addition to the work of the Commission's research coordinators, analysts and support staff, over 200 specialists from 28 universities in Canada, from the private sector and, in a number of cases, from abroad. Specialists in political science constituted the majority of our researchers, but specialists in law, economics, management, computer sciences, ethics, sociology and communications, among other disciplines, were also involved.

In addition to the preparation of research studies for the Commission, our research program included a series of research seminars, symposiums and workshops. These meetings brought together the Commissioners, researchers, representatives from the political parties, media personnel and others with practical experience in political parties, electoral politics and public affairs. These meetings provided not only a forum for discussion of the various subjects of the Commission's mandate, but also an opportunity for our research to be assessed by those with an intimate knowledge of the world of political practice.

These public reviews of our research were complemented by internal and external assessments of each research report by persons qualified in the area; such assessments were completed prior to our decision to publish any study in the series of research volumes.

The Research Branch of the Commission was divided into several areas, with the individual research projects in each area assigned to the research coordinators as follows:

| | |
|---|---|
| F. Leslie Seidle | Political Party and Election Finance |
| Herman Bakvis | Political Parties |
| Kathy Megyery | Women, Ethno-cultural Groups and Youth |
| David Small | Redistribution; Electoral Boundaries; Voter Registration |
| Janet Hiebert | Party Ethics |
| Michael Cassidy | Democratic Rights; Election Administration |
| Robert A. Milen | Aboriginal Electoral Participation and Representation |
| Frederick J. Fletcher | Mass Media and Broadcasting in Elections |
| David Mac Donald (Assistant Research Coordinator) | Direct Democracy |

These coordinators identified appropriate specialists to undertake research, managed the projects and prepared them for publication. They also organized the seminars, symposiums and workshops in their research areas and were responsible for preparing presentations and briefings to help the Commission in its deliberations and decision making. Finally, they participated in drafting the Final Report of the Commission.

On behalf of the Commission, I welcome the opportunity to thank the following for their generous assistance in producing these research studies – a project that required the talents of many individuals.

In performing their duties, the research coordinators made a notable contribution to the work of the Commission. Despite the pressures of tight deadlines, they worked with unfailing good humour and the utmost congeniality. I thank all of them for their consistent support and cooperation.

In particular, I wish to express my gratitude to Leslie Seidle, senior research coordinator, who supervised our research analysts and support staff in Ottawa. His diligence, commitment and professionalism not only set high standards, but also proved contagious. I am grateful to Kathy Megyery, who performed a similar function in Montreal with equal aplomb and skill. Her enthusiasm and dedication inspired us all.

On behalf of the research coordinators and myself, I wish to thank our research analysts: Daniel Arsenault, Eric Bertram, Cécile Boucher, Peter Constantinou, Yves Denoncourt, David Docherty, Luc Dumont, Jane Dunlop, Scott Evans, Véronique Garneau, Keith Heintzman, Paul Holmes, Hugh Mellon, Cheryl D. Mitchell, Donald Padget, Alain Pelletier, Dominique Tremblay and Lisa Young. The Research Branch was strengthened by their ability to carry out research in a wide variety of areas, their intellectual curiosity and their team spirit.

The work of the research coordinators and analysts was greatly facilitated by the professional skills and invaluable cooperation of Research Branch staff members: Paulette LeBlanc, who, as administrative assistant, managed the flow of research projects; Hélène Leroux, secretary to the research coordinators, who produced briefing material for the Commissioners and who, with Lori Nazar, assumed responsibility for monitoring the progress of research projects in the latter stages of our work; Kathleen McBride and her assistant Natalie Brose, who created and maintained the database of briefs and hearings transcripts; and Richard Herold and his assistant Susan Dancause, who were responsible for our research library. Jacinthe Séguin and Cathy Tucker also deserve thanks – in addition to their duties as receptionists, they assisted in a variety of ways to help us meet deadlines.

We were extremely fortunate to obtain the research services of first-class specialists from the academic and private sectors. Their contributions are found in this and the other 22 published research volumes. We thank them for the quality of their work and for their willingness to contribute and to meet our tight deadlines.

Our research program also benefited from the counsel of Jean-Marc Hamel, Special Adviser to the Chairman of the Commission and former

Chief Electoral Officer of Canada, whose knowledge and experience proved invaluable.

In addition, numerous specialists assessed our research studies. Their assessments not only improved the quality of our published studies, but also provided us with much-needed advice on many issues. In particular, we wish to single out professors Donald Blake, Janine Brodie, Alan Cairns, Kenneth Carty, John Courtney, Peter Desbarats, Jane Jenson, Richard Johnston, Vincent Lemieux, Terry Morley and Joseph Wearing, as well as Ms. Beth Symes.

Producing such a large number of studies in less than a year requires a mastery of the skills and logistics of publishing. We were fortunate to be able to count on the Commission's Director of Communications, Richard Rochefort, and Assistant Director, Hélène Papineau. They were ably supported by the Communications staff: Patricia Burden, Louise Dagenais, Caroline Field, Claudine Labelle, France Langlois, Lorraine Maheux, Ruth McVeigh, Chantal Morissette, Sylvie Patry, Jacques Poitras and Claudette Rouleau-O'Toole.

To bring the project to fruition, the Commission also called on specialized contractors. We are deeply grateful for the services of Ann McCoomb (references and fact checking); Marthe Lemery, Pierre Chagnon and the staff of Communications Com'ça (French quality control); Norman Bloom, Pamela Riseborough and associates of B&B Editorial Consulting (English adaptation and quality control); and Mado Reid (French production). Al Albania and his staff at Acart Graphics designed the studies and produced some 2 400 tables and figures.

The Commission's research reports constitute Canada's largest publishing project of 1991. Successful completion of the project required close cooperation between the public and private sectors. In the public sector, we especially acknowledge the excellent service of the Privy Council unit of the Translation Bureau, Department of the Secretary of State of Canada, under the direction of Michel Parent, and our contacts Ruth Steele and Terry Denovan of the Canada Communication Group, Department of Supply and Services.

The Commission's co-publisher for the research studies was Dundurn Press of Toronto, whose exceptional service is gratefully acknowledged. Wilson & Lafleur of Montreal, working with the Centre de Documentation Juridique du Québec, did equally admirable work in preparing the French version of the studies.

Teams of editors, copy editors and proofreaders worked diligently under stringent deadlines with the Commission and the publishers to prepare some 20 000 pages of manuscript for design, typesetting and printing. The work of these individuals, whose names are listed elsewhere in this volume, was greatly appreciated.

Our acknowledgements extend to the contributions of the Commission's Executive Director, Guy Goulard, and the administration and executive support teams: Maurice Lacasse, Denis Lafrance and Steve Tremblay (finance); Thérèse Lacasse and Mary Guy-Shea (personnel); Cécile Desforges (assistant to the Executive Director); Marie Dionne (administration); Anna Bevilacqua (records); and support staff members Michelle Bélanger, Roch Langlois, Michel Lauzon, Jean Mathieu, David McKay and Pierrette McMurtie, as well as Denise Miquelon and Christiane Séguin of the Montreal office.

A special debt of gratitude is owed to Marlène Girard, assistant to the Chairman. Her ability to supervise the logistics of the Commission's work amid the tight schedules of the Chairman and Commissioners contributed greatly to the completion of our task.

I also wish to express my deep gratitude to my own secretary, Liette Simard. Her superb administrative skills and great patience brought much-appreciated order to my penchant for the chaotic workstyle of academe. She also assumed responsibility for the administrative coordination of revisions to the final drafts of volumes 1 and 2 of the Commission's Final Report. I owe much to her efforts and assistance.

Finally, on behalf of the research coordinators and myself, I wish to thank the Chairman, Pierre Lortie, the members of the Commission, Pierre Fortier, Robert Gabor, William Knight and Lucie Pépin, and former members Elwood Cowley and Senator Donald Oliver. We are honoured to have worked with such an eminent and thoughtful group of Canadians, and we have benefited immensely from their knowledge and experience. In particular, we wish to acknowledge the creativity, intellectual rigour and energy our Chairman brought to our task. His unparalleled capacity to challenge, to bring out the best in us, was indeed inspiring.

Peter Aucoin
Director of Research

# PREFACE

IN MODERN DEMOCRACIES, election campaigns are contested to a large extent in the mass media. While the right to vote freely and the credibility of the ballot process are central to democracy, the conduct of campaigns and the flow of information to voters are also significant. In recent elections, published opinion polls have come to be an important, and controversial, part of the information made available to voters by the news media.

This volume is one of six in the Royal Commission's research series dealing with electoral communication. Like the other studies, it is concerned not only with technical matters but also with issues of fairness in electoral competition and public confidence in the electoral process. In addition, like much of the research reported in these volumes, it has an important comparative dimension. The study was initiated because of concerns raised in the public hearings of the Commission about published opinion polls.

As Albert Cantril (1991) noted in a recent book on public polling in the United States, polls are undergoing a crisis of legitimacy. Although doubts about their general reliability have been dispelled, increasingly questions are raised about their role in electoral politics. These questions stem from a conviction that polls do influence election campaigns, promoting strategic voting, stimulating bandwagon effects (which now appear to be documented in several countries) and, in particular, influencing party fund-raising, the morale of party workers and media coverage.

In this volume, Guy Lachapelle presents a comprehensive overview of published campaign polls in many democratic countries. He reports that, while direct regulation of polls is rare, there is growing concern about their influence. The study examines regulations now in place and others that have been proposed. The most common rules involve disclosure of technical information and blackout periods during which poll data cannot be published. In addition to formal regulation, Professor Lachapelle has examined the professional codes of the World Association for Public Opinion Research (WAPOR) and of many national organizations, including those formulated by news organizations. He discusses the attempts of polling organizations and the news media to establish mechanisms of self-regulation.

In a close examination of the Canadian scene during the 1988 federal election campaign, he found that the number of published polls has been increasing. There were 22 national polls published during the eight-week campaign in 1988, nearly twice the number published in 1984, but still far short of the 73 in the British election of 1987 or the scores of polls in the 1988 U.S. presidential election.

At the heart of the study is an examination of the reports provided by pollsters to the media for most of the national polls and the actual daily newspaper reporting of those polls (and of 37 regional and local polls). He found that important technical information was missing not only from news reports but also from the reports provided to the media. The media reports, in many cases, did not live up to the professional codes or style books of their own organizations. He concludes that voters would be hard-pressed to assess the technical soundness of many of them. More important, the information needed to promote public debate among pollsters and other experts was lacking from the news reports.

The author recommends that the media be required by law to publish specified technical information, that pollsters make more efforts to educate journalists and that there be a blackout on publication of polls during the final three days of the campaign. With respect to the blackout, he argues that it would permit candidates to respond to controversial or misleading polls before the vote.

The study makes important contributions to the study of published opinion polling in several areas. First, it presents a comprehensive survey of regulations regarding election polling in democracies, information not readily available anywhere else. Second, the study examines professional codes of conduct developed by several associations of polling organizations. Third, it discusses the norms found in professional codes and media style books regarding the reporting of polls. Fourth, it offers a critique of the actual reporting of polls. The information and analysis in this volume will make a lasting contribution to the study of media polling.

The Commission's research program on mass media and elections drew on the expertise of a wide range of communication scholars and political scientists. Their contributions are acknowledged in other volumes. On behalf of the author and the Commission, I must also acknowledge our debt to the practitioners from the news media, the parties and the polling organizations, who attended our seminars and provided constructive comments on this and other studies. This study also benefited from the conscientious work of anonymous peer reviewers.

The administration of the research program depended heavily on Cheryl Mitchell, who served as my assistant from the inception of the program and helped to edit this study among others. My assistants at York University were also very helpful. Professor Lachapelle deserves special acknowledgement for his conscientious efforts to respond to the comments we provided to him.

The unfailing good humour and encouragement of Peter Aucoin, the director of research, made an important contribution to the work. It was a privilege to work with the Commissioners, whose willingness to bring their experience to bear on the most esoteric of formulations was an inspiration. Pierre Lortie's overall direction and, in particular, his suggestions for research and incisive comments on various drafts made a vital contribution, which is reflected in these research volumes as well as in the Final Report of the Royal Commission. Richard Rochefort and his staff were crucial in bringing these studies to publication.

On a personal note, I wish to thank my wife and frequent collaborator, Martha Fletcher, for encouraging me to undertake this task, which I have found very rewarding, and for her direct advice on many aspects of the work, as well as for bearing more than her share of the burden of domestic management. My son, Frederick, reminded me that work, however important, must be balanced with other aspects of life and that the future of the democratic process is worth working for.

Fred Fletcher
Research Coordinator

# ACKNOWLEDGEMENTS

THIS STUDY WOULD not have been possible without the contributions of many people. I particularly want to thank André Turcotte, who reviewed and commented on numerous drafts. Our many discussions and his extremely helpful remarks meant that I could count on a critical eye throughout the process. Caroline Roy offered her expertise in analysing Canadian legislation. I cannot overlook the very useful and detailed observations by Frederick J. Fletcher, Cheryl D. Mitchell and two anonymous evaluators, without whose assistance this final version would not be what it is. Nor can I leave out Gail Trottier, who took care of word processing the manuscript.

Finally, this study would never have been completed without the support of Lyne Lalonde, pharmacist and part-time political analyst, or without the good humour of our children, Marc-Olivier and Camille.

Guy Lachapelle

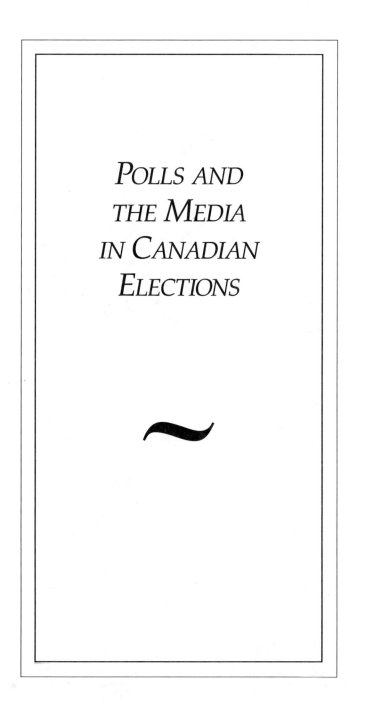

# POLLS AND
# THE MEDIA
# IN CANADIAN
# ELECTIONS

# 1

# INTRODUCTION
## Polls and
## Democracy

~

IN CANADA, as in most Western democracies, polls have become an important election phenomenon, proliferating steadily during various elections over the past decade. Twenty-two country-wide polls were conducted during the 1988 Canadian federal election. In addition there were 37 polls in particular constituencies, metropolitan areas, regions, provinces, groups of constituencies or target populations. These are only the polls whose results were released in the daily and weekly press. During the 1988 presidential election in France, the polling commission listed and monitored 153 polls, compared with 111 in 1981, for an increase of 39 percent. The numbers were also very high for the American presidential race in 1988. In England during the 1987 election, the number of national polls (40) increased considerably, but a new phenomenon also appeared: constituency polling. Between the 1984 and 1987 British elections, the number of constituency polls rose from 40 to 78, excluding the other types of polls.

Polls are multiplying and collecting at newsroom doors. Journalists have participated in this phenomenon to the point where the role of polling in a democracy is increasingly controversial. Although some people would like polls to be treated like any other information, others are increasingly realizing that journalists must have specialized skills to report and analyse polls accurately. Journalists' associations and broadcasters have adopted codes of ethics and interpretation with respect to polls – attesting to the fact that polls represent a specific type of information, and that journalistic treatment must be accompanied by certain basic data. Of course, the entire issue of regulating polling during and outside of election periods is debatable. Some people fear any form of state intervention, polls being but a pretext for control of political information and journalistic practice.

The most recent quasi-experimental studies set out to verify what, until then, had been but a vague theory: that polls do, in fact, influence voter behaviour, particularly voting intentions (Ceci and Kain 1982; Marsh 1984; Cloutier et al. 1989). The preliminary results of the research on the 1988 Canadian election (Canadian National Election Study 1988) show that the behaviour of some voters is guided partly *but not solely* by the published and broadcast results of polls (Blais et al. 1990). Poll results could not only have a bandwagon effect but could also influence each voter's selection of a particular candidate or party. The theory of public choice proposes a new vision of a voter: no longer an apathetic recipient, bombarded by polls, but an individual capable of diverse reactions to information stimuli. Various voter behaviours (cyclical, strategic, monotonic) are possible and can change the course of an election (Johnson 1991, 217–20). Strangely enough, those who once advocated regulating polls because they influence ill-informed or undecided voters still maintain the same position – polls provoke unexpected reactions that in some way distort the democratic process (Johnson 1991).

The objective of this study is not to resolve all these issues but to make a modest contribution to a better understanding of polls as a source of information for voters. Journalistic treatment of polls remains a key issue in Western democracies, especially in Canada. Since we consider polls as information that is primarily scientific, our conclusions could not apply to all the political or partisan information broadcast during election campaigns. Our first objective was, thus, to determine how this technical information is presented in the Canadian media and to see if we could detect strengths or weaknesses that would restrict the public's right to reliable information. Of course the information cannot be perfect, but it can certainly be improved. Adherence to ethical or methodological standards cannot by itself guarantee free debate in a democratic society. However, the media and journalists can ensure that all information contained in polls receives full public discussion and examination.

This study therefore has a specific objective: to provide as broad and accurate an overview as possible of what the chair of the French polling commission calls the "polling landscape" in Canada. To do this, we set various sub-objectives:

- to analyse the comments and recommendations of various interveners who submitted briefs to the Royal Commission on Electoral Reform and Party Financing;
- to examine the legislation that regulates polling, as well as court decisions that circumscribe its use;

- to compare Canada with various countries that have regulated polling completely, partially or not at all;
- to see what ethical and methodological standards the main actors – researchers, pollsters, journalists, broadcasters and governments – have established to regulate this activity; and
- to examine how polling organizations, the media and broadcasters actually dealt with polls during the 1988 federal election and whether they observed certain polling rules.

Our analysis will therefore deal only with the tip of the iceberg. Many channels of communication beyond public opinion polls influence voters and spread information. Polls conducted by political parties are, from this viewpoint, one very important aspect of the whole election strategy, targeted specifically at certain partisan or citizen groups. Nevertheless, we will have achieved our goal if this study encourages public discussion on an important aspect of modern democracies.

## POLLING: A SCIENCE

For the historian of scientific surveys, there are at least three stages in the development of methods for gathering public opinion. The first includes all efforts to acknowledge and integrate the significant role public opinion can play in political governance. In ancient Athens, Pericles gathered his compatriots to discuss the problems of the city-state; because they were few in number, each could take part in the debate. It was not until 2 May 1744 that Jean-Jacques Rousseau used the term "public opinion" for the first time in its modern sense, when he was France's foreign affairs secretary (Noelle-Neumann 1984, chap. 7). This first stage was characterized mainly by the constant search for a definition of the nature of public opinion and its relationship with political authority.

The second stage, characterized by efforts to survey a greater number of people to determine their opinions, began with the publication of the first straw poll (Robinson 1932) in two Pennsylvania newspapers, the *Harrisburg Pennsylvanian* and the *Raleigh Star*, during the 1824 presidential election. In the summer of 1824, this survey gave 335 votes to Andrew Jackson, 169 to John Quincy Adams, 19 to Henry Clay and 9 to William H. Crawford. Later the same year, the *Raleigh Star* conducted another survey among 4 256 citizens during public meetings in North Carolina. This poll, too, put Jackson ahead. However, Adams won the election and Jackson had to wait another four years to be elected to the presidency of the United States. According to Stoetzel and Girard (1973, 41), it was during this period that the press first became aware of the concept of "opinion news." Previously, only those in power concerned themselves with public opinion; now journalists had various means to monitor the pulse of the nation: "Voting intentions are sought by the most varied means imaginable: ballots in newspapers to be filled in, clipped out and returned; postcards mailed to addresses taken from telephone books; mail boxes and even 'polling stations' set up in busy parts of town; and reporters questioning passers-by" (ibid., 40–41).

Despite its lack of reliability, the straw poll took a long time to disappear. In 1833, Charles H. Taylor, publisher of the *Boston Globe*, assigned reporters to cover specific electoral districts – a system that is used by television networks today. In 1904, the *New York Herald* questioned 30 000 voters in New York City. In the presidential elections of 1908 and 1912, the *New York Herald* entered into an association with the *Cincinnati Enquirer*, the *Chicago Record-Herald*, the *St. Louis Republic*, the *Boston Globe* and the *Los Angeles Times*. However, this attempt to predict voting intentions had only limited success.

For example, the *Literary Digest* began conducting surveys in 1916 when it sent 11 million postcards to telephone subscribers. In 1920, the target population for this type of survey increased to 16.5 million people: cards were sent to car owners as well as telephone subscribers. This survey procedure was again used during the elections of 1936 and 1940.

In 1936, the *Literary Digest* published a straw poll after sending out 10 million postcards and examining responses from at least 2.4 million people; the results predicted that President Franklin D. Roosevelt would be defeated. He was, in fact, re-elected. This spectacular failure resulted from the sampling method used: the *Literary Digest* had used the addresses of individuals who owned telephones and cars – a group clearly wealthier and less favourable to Roosevelt's policies. Gallup, Roper and Crossley began conducting opinion polls that same year, using their own sampling methods. All three pollsters predicted a victory for Roosevelt.

Closer to home, British Columbia adopted legislation in 1939 prohibiting any individual, corporation or organization from taking a poll during an election period. In the 1972 provincial election, however, the results of some polls were widely publicized by the media. For example, one restaurant decided to wrap its hamburgers in paper in the traditional colours of the main political parties: blue for the Conservatives, red for the Liberals, green for the New Democrats, and white for the Social Credit party. The idea of the "hamburger survey" was to predict the election outcome by counting the number of "Barrettburgers" and "Bennettburgers" sold. Customers played the game willingly, and the media gave the results wide coverage (Cloutier 1982, 7).

The third stage began with the idea of using representative sampling techniques to isolate sections of a given population. This technique was developed by the Norwegian statistician A.N. Kiaer. During the course of heated discussions within the International Institute of Statistics in 1895, 1897 and 1901, Kiaer finally convinced his colleagues of the merits of this approach. Thus, in 1903, the Institute recommended the use of the method, "provided that in the presentation of results, the conditions used to select the units observed are spelled out in their entirety" [translation]. Already, we can see that the members felt it necessary to take precautions and to specify the sampling method used. Then, in 1925, subsequent to a report by Denmark's A. Jensen, the Institute reaffirmed its 1903 recommendation (*Institut international de statistique* 1926).

The technique owes its commercial application to Americans Archibald Crossley and Elmo Roper, who conducted the first scientific public opinion poll in 1936, the same year that George Gallup conducted his first poll. By questioning between 4 000 and 5 000 people, each pollster predicted correctly that Roosevelt would be elected, although Gallup underestimated the extent of Roosevelt's victory by 6.8 percent.

Gallup opened an office in London in 1936, thereby making the British Institute of Public Opinion (Gallup) the first body in England to conduct a poll as we understand the term today. The results of the British surveys were published in the *News Chronicle*, which closed its doors in 1960. Since that time, Gallup survey results in England have appeared regularly in the *Daily Telegraph*. A question about the degree of satisfaction with the government was first introduced in October 1937; this was followed by the first question on voting intentions in February 1939 (Worcester 1984, 1991). Only Gallup conducted polls during the 1945 British election.

In 1941, George Gallup founded institutes in Australia and Canada as well. The Canadian Institute of Public Opinion, however, would face a uniquely Canadian problem: that of drafting questionnaires in both French and English and ensuring that the questions were similar and equivalent (Sanders 1943). Wilfrid Sanders became the first Canadian Co-Director of Gallup Canada in 1941; other well-known individuals, including the French political scientist Alfred Max, were also among the first to work for Gallup.

The 1948 U.S. presidential election was a real fiasco for polling firms. Gallup, Crossley and Roper all predicted that Thomas E. Dewey would defeat Harry S Truman (who was running for a second term) by 49.5 to 44.5, 49.9 to 44.8 and 52.2 to 37.1 percent, respectively. The results were quite the opposite. Truman got 49.5 percent of the vote, while his opponent garnered 45.1 percent. The Social Sciences Research Council studied these polls extensively and examined the reasons for their failure, identifying five main causes (Mosteller et al. 1949, appendix A):

1. The pollsters stopped interviewing too soon and combined results from the beginning and the end of the campaign; thus, they were unable to take into account the strong last-minute swing to Truman.
2. The sample design resulted in an overestimation of electors with middle and high incomes (the latter have a greater tendency to vote Republican).
3. The methods used were not sufficiently reliable to predict whether respondents actually intended to vote on election day.
4. The polling organizations had not yet settled on a method of allotting undecided voters to the various candidates.
5. Because of a chance factor, the random selection method used caused sample results to vary from the results obtained for the population as a whole.

Polls accurately predicted the outcome of the 1950 British election, despite public scepticism arising from the spectacular failure of the Dewey–Truman polls. Political scientists Butler and Rose believed that polls had relatively little influence on voters in England prior to the 1960s: "It does not appear that people jump on to the winning band-wagon – or even that they side with the underdog ... It is also true that the turnout may be increased by signs that the rivals are neck-and-neck ... the effect of the polls, like that of television, seems to be to stir up interest, and hence participation in the election" (Butler and Rose 1960, 106).

These authors also stressed the importance of educating the public about polls and of having pollsters reveal more information on how their polls are conducted: "What is also needed is a higher degree of education about the limitations and possibilities of the polls and perhaps more information and humility from some of their sponsors. The first thing that has to be learnt is that their main value does not lie primarily in election prediction" (Butler and Rose 1960, 107).

It was not until the early 1960s that the use of polls during elections became common practice in England. Between 1945 and 1987, the results of some 55 polls were printed and distributed during the last few days of each election campaign (see table 1.1). Generally speaking, British election polls have been fairly accurate, although they have tended to underestimate the Conservative vote and to overestimate the Labour vote. However, in the early 1970s a new phenomenon appeared: advocacy polling. Advocacy polls are sponsored by interest groups; polling firms were concerned about this practice both because they feared their reputation might suffer and because the media were sceptical of the results of this type of survey.

Table 1.1
**Number of polls published during British election campaigns and margins of error**

| Election year | Mean margin of error | Mean margin of error by party | Number of polls |
|---|---|---|---|
| 1945 | 3.5 | 1.5 | 1 |
| 1950 | 4.6 | 1.7 | 3 |
| 1951 | 5.3 | 2.2 | 3 |
| 1955 | 0.2 | 0.9 | 2 |
| 1959 | 1.1 | 0.8 | 4 |
| 1964 | 0.8 | 1.5 | 4 |
| 1966 | 3.9 | 1.5 | 4 |
| 1970 | 6.6 | 2.2 | 5 |
| 1974 February | 2.4 | 1.6 | 6 |
| 1974 October | 5.0 | 1.6 | 6 |
| 1979 | 1.7 | 0.9 | 5 |
| 1983 | 4.3 | 1.1 | 6 |
| 1987 | 3.2 | 1.2 | 6 |
| Mean | 3.3 | 1.4 | |
| N | | | 55 |

Source: Worcester (1991, 110).

The figures quoted earlier are not a completely accurate reflection of polling practice in England, as they do not take into account surveys published during election campaigns. According to Butler and Kavanagh (1984, 127), at least 50 polls were taken during the 1983 election, and 39 national surveys were conducted during the last five weeks of the 1987 campaign (see table 1.2).[1] Where British national polls are concerned, however, we should make a clear distinction between regional polls, marginal polls (conducted in hotly contested ridings), constituency polls (conducted in certain ridings only), and polls sponsored by political parties. Accordingly, Robert Worcester (1991) identified seven polls taken in Scotland, one in Wales, approximately a dozen regional polls, and 40 to 50 polls taken on behalf of political parties during the 1987 campaign.

Marginal polls are a recent phenomenon in England, although Gallup conducted the first poll of this type during the 1959 election. A

Table 1.2
National polls conducted during the 1987 British election: voting intention

| Week | Number of polls | Conservative (%) | Labour (%) | Liberal–SDP (%) |
|---|---|---|---|---|
| 11–17 May | 5 | 42.0 | 31.0 | 25.0 |
| 18–24 May | 8 | 42.0 | 34.0 | 22.0 |
| 25–31 May | 9 | 43.0 | 34.0 | 21.0 |
| 1–7 June | 9 | 43.0 | 34.0 | 21.5 |
| 8–11 June | 8 | 42.0 | 34.0 | 22.0 |
| Total | 39 | | | |
| Mean | | 42.4 | 33.4 | 22.3 |
| Election results | | 43.3 | 31.5 | 23.1 |

Source: Norris (1989, 224).

Note: Percentages do not add to 100.0 because of rounding.

median point established in accordance with various criteria is used as a basis for selecting the ridings most likely to swing to another party (see Norris 1989, chap. 20). In 1983, only the Harris firm took marginal polls, and that was for *Weekend World* (15, 22 and 29 May 1983). In 1987, the number of marginal polls rose to 20. In addition, 78 constituency polls involving 52 ridings were conducted; at least 15 polling institutes carried out this type of survey (Waller 1989, chap. 21).

## THE CANADIAN EXPERIENCE

In England, the media are the main sponsors of polls during elections. The Canadian media do not sponsor as many polls as their British counterparts, doubtless for financial reasons. During the 1983 British and 1984 Canadian elections, the British media sponsored 47 polls over the 30 days of the campaign (Butler and Kavanagh 1984, 127), whereas the Canadian media sponsored only 12 over the 58 days of the campaign. However, during the 1988 Canadian federal election, 22 national polls and no fewer than 37 regional, provincial, constituency, issue and party polls were conducted.

The development of polling in Canada is essentially similar to the British experience. During the 1945 general election, the Canadian Institute of Public Opinion conducted the first election poll, but it was only during the 1960s that opinion polling really began to take flight. The first poll in Canada had been conducted by the Liberal Party of Canada in 1942, when the Mackenzie King government attempted to determine the likely outcome of a forthcoming plebiscite on conscription (Magnant 1980, 19). John Meisel and Peter Regenstrief, however, were the first to conduct true sociological surveys of Canadian public opinion. In Quebec, the first political poll was conducted in 1959 by the Groupe de recherche sociale (Social research group) for the Quebec Liberal party on the eve of the 1960 provincial election. Jean Lesage was also one of the first party leaders to develop an electoral strategy on the basis of poll results. However, it was only during the 1965 federal election that election polling really took off in the Canadian press.

Canada's major polling institutes, founded between 1965 and 1980, include Goldfarb Consultants, Canadian Facts (Réalités canadiennes), Sorécom (Société de recherches en sciences du comportement), Decima Research, Data Laboratories, Thompson-Lightstone, CROP (Centre de recherche sur l'opinion publique) and the IQOP (Institut québécois d'opinion publique).

Polling has become so widespread in Canada that many people fear that it has acquired undue influence over governments and voters. Although it would be difficult to prove whether there are grounds for such concern, there may be a need to regulate the practice. In this study, we will attempt to clarify some of the limits of the *Canada Elections Act* by comparing Canadian legislation with that in other countries; examine the codes of conduct and ethical standards existing in Canada; and determine whether these standards were adhered to by polling organizations and the media during the last federal election. We will also analyse journalistic treatment of regional, local, constituency, issue and party polls. Finally, we will examine the kinds of rules that could be established to regulate polls in Canada.

# 2

## CANADIANS AND PUBLIC OPINION POLLS
### *An Examination of the Proposals Submitted to the Commission*

THE EFFECT OF POLLS during election periods remains a subject of controversy and public concern. Of all the issues discussed before the Royal Commission on Electoral Reform and Party Financing, the issue of regulating polls during elections was among those that inspired many suggestions from political parties and organizations, the media, pollsters, researchers, interest groups and individuals. At least 90 briefs presented to the Commission dealt with the influence of polls during elections and suggested various models for regulation. The basic argument of most of these briefs was that polls have undue influence on election campaigns, especially a potential influence on voters. The purpose of this chapter will therefore be to summarize these presentations in an attempt to define the range of opinions on polling in Canada.

Various interveners mentioned several effects of opinion polls on voters at election time:

- the bandwagon effect (electors rally to support the candidate leading in the polls);
- the underdog effect (electors rally to support the candidate trailing in the polls);
- the demotivating effect (electors abstain from voting out of certainty that their candidate will win);
- the motivating effect (electors vote because the polls alert them to the fact that an election is going on);
- the strategic effect (electors decide how to vote on the basis of the

relative popularity of the parties according to the polls); and
- the free-will effect (electors vote to prove the polls wrong).[2]

However, no definitive conclusion about the actual impact of polls on voters can be drawn from these briefs. This is a matter of controversy even among researchers.

The theory of party decline was also mentioned by some interveners. According to this theory, the main effect of opinion polls during elections has been to reduce the campaign role of party workers and the candidate's obligation to find out more about people's real needs (Meisel 1985, 106). Establishing influential networks and close ties among candidates, local groups and party organizations is now not as important as having party strategists who can rapidly weigh the relative importance of various groups and, thus, decide how much public exposure to give candidates and party leaders. Furthermore, the role of the grassroots worker at the constituency level – both as a link between the public and various party authorities and as a valuable source of local information – has increasingly been devalued and even reduced. Consequently, opinion polls, among other things, have replaced the local party organization as a line of communication between the public and their elected representatives.

Although some analysts believe that certain voters are likely to be influenced by opinion polls and that polls have a negative influence on grassroots party organizations, these propositions remain contested. The impact of polls on party strategy and party organization is widely accepted but also not fully verified. Nevertheless, it is important to ensure that the data publicized are reliable, no matter what their impact. The public's right to accurate information, which is a basic democratic principle in pluralistic societies, remains the cornerstone of any attempt to judge the validity and the scientific value of polls. If polls are used improperly and left in the hands of virtually anyone claiming to be qualified to conduct them, democracy will be the loser. We can learn something from France, where the Commission des sondages (polling commission) has been able to prevent certain firms from using questionable methods.

Elections are decisive moments in a country's democratic life, and all electoral and partisan information, including polls, should at the very least encourage public debate on the choice of elected representatives, the operation of public institutions and organizations, and the management of government policies. Polls are just one of the many tools used to reveal public opinion. They may encourage public debate by making it possible for voters and citizens to compare their opinions with those of the majority on a multitude of issues. The main challenge for polling organizations and journalists is to ensure that the questions asked and the data published or broadcast are pertinent and valid. Information thus plays a vital role during election campaigns; it must be accurate to enable voters to make sound decisions and at the same time encourage public debate.

A number of briefs also dealt with respect for democratic principles and the various means legislators have at their disposal to regulate polls and promote adherence to these principles, albeit without becoming too interventionist. Various questions on polling during and outside election periods arose:

- Should opinion polls be prohibited during elections, or at least for a certain part of the campaign?
- Should the media be asked to publish or broadcast technical and methodological information with the poll results to enable the public to judge the quality and reliability of such polls?
- Should the reports that accompany polls be made accessible to the public?
- Should exit polls (polls of those leaving a voting booth) be prohibited?
- Should a polling commission independent of Elections Canada be created? Alternatively, should polling organizations be asked to send the Chief Electoral Officer of Canada all data pertaining to the production of opinion polls during an election campaign?
- Would it be preferable to count on self-regulation by researchers, pollsters and the media or to decide firmly in favour of a laissez-faire approach?

This study will attempt to respond to all of these questions. But first, let us see how Canadians have answered them.

### SELF-REGULATION, GOVERNMENT REGULATION OR LAISSEZ-FAIRE?

Legislators can choose from among three options to regulate polling during and outside election periods. Self-regulation would leave it up to the participants, particularly the media and polling organizations, to regulate their own professions and to ensure that certain basic ethical standards are respected. The main responsibility would fall to pollsters and journalists. Pollsters would have to establish their own code of conduct. Journalists would have to ensure that the public was accurately informed by presenting and commenting on poll data responsibly and appropriately. In a free market or laissez-faire situation, competition among polling institutes would oblige them to produce higher-quality polls, at the same time forcing self-regulation. In this case, organizations with dubious qualifications would soon be exposed.

Government regulation is obviously still an option that some would qualify as élitist, especially if it is based on the notion that opinion polls influence the public and that this influence must be limited. Government regulation is also seen as the first step toward political despotism; making decision makers responsible for determining what can or cannot be published could represent a threat to democracy. It is also considered costly, as any government intervention means a greater degree of bureaucracy. Despite such criticisms, however, some governments have chosen to go this route over the past few years, as we will see in the section on legislation.

Sixty-three (70 percent) of the 90 briefs submitted to the Commission favoured government regulation of polls during elections, 22 (24.4 percent) favoured laissez-faire, and only three (3.3 percent) opted for self-regulation. One intervener suggested that the government give polling organizations two years to establish a code of ethics, after which time legislators could decide whether the corrective measures taken were sufficient or if government regulation was indeed necessary. Only one person suggested that the Commission instead study the effect of polls at election time. Despite considerable public support for government regulation, not everyone has the same perspective on the attendant issues. Interveners focused on four of these: the length of the restriction period, including a blackout; the presentation of the survey specifications sheet; the question of exit polls; and the idea of polls being included as election expenses.

In the following pages we look briefly at each of these issues. We prefer to look at how the various interveners – political parties, MPs and senators, journalists and broadcasters, pollsters and researchers, interest groups and ordinary citizens – dealt with the issues. It might have been more logical to discuss each theme separately; however, we believe that our approach, though less systematic, gives a better picture of Canadians' attitudes toward polling. At the same time, it enables us to compare the positions taken by the various interveners. The position of each intervener is summarized in table 1.3.

### Political Parties and Associations

There are significant differences among the groups that submitted briefs to the Commission. It is also rather surprising to note that, whereas the national leadership of the three major parties (the Progressive Conservative Party of Canada, the Liberal Party of Canada and the New

**Table 1.3**
**Summary of proposals to regulate polls during election periods**

| Intervener | Type of intervention[a] | Restriction period | Survey specifications sheet[b] (s. 98.1, Bill C-79) | Exit polls | Election expenses[c] |
|---|---|---|---|---|---|
| **Parties, political associations, MPs and senators** | | | | | |
| 1. *Progressive Conservative Party of Canada* | | | | | |
| Progressive Conservative Party of Canada | Laissez-faire | | Opposed s. 98.1 | | |
| Progressive Conservative Association of PEI | Government | Last few days | | | |
| Association progressiste-conservatrice de Roberval (Que.) | Government | | | | |
| Progressive Conservative Association of Thompson (Man.–Sask.) | Government | | | | |
| Progressive Conservative Association of Regina–Wascana (Man.–Sask.) | Laissez-faire | | Yes | | |
| Progressive Conservative Association of Churchill (Man.–Sask.) | Laissez-faire | | | | |
| Progressive Conservative Association of Capilano–Howe Sound (BC–YT) | Government | | | | |
| Progressive Conservative Association of Vancouver Island | Government | | | | |
| Larry Grossman, former leader of the Ontario party | Government | Entire campaign | | | |

**Table 1.3** (cont'd)
**Summary of proposals to regulate polls during election periods**

| Intervener | Type of intervention[a] | Restriction period | Survey specifications sheet[b] (s. 98.1, Bill C-79) | Exit polls | Election expenses[c] |
|---|---|---|---|---|---|
| 2. *Liberal Party of Canada* | | | | | |
| Liberal Party of Canada | Laissez-faire | | Opposed 98.1 | | Yes |
| Liberal Party of Canada, Quebec section | Government | 10 days | | | |
| Liberal Party of Canada, BC section | Government | Entire campaign | | | |
| Kamloops Liberal Association (BC) | Government | Entire campaign | | | |
| Federal Liberal Association of Saanich–Gulf Islands (BC) | Government | 4 weeks | | | |
| Liberal Party of Canada, Alberta section | Government | | Yes | | |
| Saskatoon–Dundurn Liberal Association | Government | 72 hours | Yes | | |
| Liberal Association of Nova Scotia | Government | 2 weeks | Yes | | |
| Liberal Association of Prince Edward Island | Government | | | | |
| Brant Federal Liberal Association (Ont.) | Government | Mid-campaign | | | |
| Federal Liberal Association of the Yukon | Government | | Yes | | |

**Table 1.3** (cont'c)
**Summary of proposals to regulate polls during election periods**

| Intervener | Type of intervention[a] | Restriction period | Survey specifications sheet[b] (s. 98.1, Bill C-79) | Exit polls | Election expenses[c] |
|---|---|---|---|---|---|
| **3. New Democratic Party** | | | | | |
| New Democratic Party of Canada | Laissez-faire | | | | Yes |
| New Democrats of Saskatchewan | Government | | Yes | | |
| New Democratic Party, PEI | Government | 2 weeks | | | |
| New Democrat Association of Burnaby–Kingsway (BC–YT) | Government | Entire campaign | | | |
| New Democrats of the Provincial Riding of Sudbury (Ont.) | Government | Entire campaign | | | |
| **4. Other parties** | | | | | |
| Parti nationaliste du Québec | Government | | Yes | | |
| Green Party of Canada, Niagara Falls (Ont.) | Government | | Yes | | |
| Rhinoceros Party | Laissez-faire | | | | |
| Confederation of Regions Western Party | Government | Entire campaign or 90 days | | | |

Table 1.3 (cont'd)
**Summary of proposals to regulate polls during election periods**

| Intervener | Type of intervention[a] | Restriction period | Survey specifications sheet[b] (s. 98.1, Bill C-79) | Exit polls | Election expenses[c] |
|---|---|---|---|---|---|
| **5.  *MPs, senators, former MPs and candidates*** | | | | | |
| Norman Atkins, Senator | Government | | Yes | | |
| Nelson Riis, MP (Kamloops) | Government | | Yes | | |
| Howard Crosby, MP (Halifax West) | Government | | Yes | | |
| Atul Kapur, NDP candidate | Government | Entire campaign | | | |
| Steve Whipp, NDP candidate | Government | | | Yes (U.S. media) | |
| Cyril Keeper, former Winnipeg MP | Laissez-faire | Short period | | | |
| Don Ferguson, NDP candidate | Undecided | | | | |
| Judy Whitaker, NDP candidate | Government | | | | |
| **Other interveners** | | | | | |
| **6.  *Journalists and broadcasters*** | | | | | |
| Quebec Federation of Professional Journalists | Self-regulation | 48 hours | Opposed s. 98.1 | Yes | |
| Association canadienne de la radio et de la télévision de langue française | Laissez-faire | 48 hours | | Yes | |

**Table 1.3 (cont'd)**
**Summary of proposals to regulate polls during election periods**

| Intervener | Type of intervention[a] | Restriction period | Survey specifications sheet[b] (s. 98.1, Bill C-79) | Exit polls | Election expenses[c] |
|---|---|---|---|---|---|
| Canadian Association of Broadcasters | Laissez-faire | | | | |
| CTV Television Network | Laissez-faire | | | | |
| CBC / Société Radio-Canada | Self-regulation | | | | |
| VOCM Radio (St. John's, Nfld.) | Laissez-faire | | Yes | | |
| CJPM-TV, CKRS and CKRS-TV, CHRL-Radio (Chicoutimi, Que.) | Laissez-faire | | | | |
| 7. *Pollsters and researchers* | | | | | |
| Sorécom Inc. | Self-regulation | | | | |
| Angus Reid and Associates | Laissez-faire | | | Yes | |
| Environics Research Group Ltd. | Laissez-faire | | | | |
| Gallup Canada Inc. | Laissez-faire | | | | |
| Omnifacts Research Ltd. | Government | 24 hours | Yes | Yes | |
| Comité des sondages du regroupement québécois des sciences sociales | Government | | Yes | | |
| Vincent Lemieux (Université Laval) | Laissez-faire | | | | |
| Agar Adamson (Acadia University) | Self-regulation and government | 2 weeks | | | |
| Howard Leeson, Ray Sentas, Lorne Brown, Gerry Sperling, Dan de Vlieger (Man.–Sask.) | Government | Entire campaign | | | |

Table 1.3 (cont'd)
**Summary of proposals to regulate polls during election periods**

| Intervener | Type of intervention[a] | Restriction period | Survey specifications sheet[b] (s. 98.1, Bill C-79) | Exit polls | Election expenses[c] |
|---|---|---|---|---|---|
| **8. Interest groups** | | | | | |
| Concerned Citizens for Civic Affairs in North York | Laissez-faire | | | | |
| Citizens Concerned about Free Trade | Government | | | | Yes |
| Saskatchewan Association of Rural Municipalities | Government | Entire campaign | | | |
| Moncton Chamber of Commerce | Government | Mid-campaign | | | |
| Thompson Chamber of Commerce (Man.–Sask.) | Laissez-faire | | | | |
| Calgary Chamber of Commerce | Government | | Yes | | |
| Canadian Home and School and Parent-Teacher Federation | Government | Entire campaign | Yes | | |
| Institute for Political Involvement | Laissez-faire | | | | |
| Ontario Advisory Council for Disabled Persons | Government | | | | |
| Tribal Council of the Dakota–Ojibwa | Government | Entire campaign | | | |
| Manitoba Keewatinowi Okimakanik Inc. | Government | | Yes | | |
| BC Civil Liberties Association | Laissez-faire | | | | |

**Table 1.3** (cont'd)
**Summary of proposals to regulate polls during election periods**

| Intervener | Type of intervention[a] | Restriction period | Survey specifications sheet[b] (s. 98.1, Bill C-79) | Exit polls | Election expenses[c] |
|---|---|---|---|---|---|
| 9. *Individual citizens* | | | | | |
| Garfield Warren (Nfld.) | Government | Entire campaign | | | |
| Bertrand Tremblay (Que.) | Government | 2 weeks | | | |
| Jean Cadieux (Maritimes) | Government | 10 days | | | |
| Daniel Beamish (Ont.) | Government | Entire campaign | | | |
| Margaret Blair (Ont.) | Government | | Yes | | |
| David J. Carll (Ont.) | Government | 2 weeks | | | |
| David B. Fogarty (Ont.) | Government | | Yes | | |
| R. Harvey Self (Ont.) | Government | Entire campaign | | | |
| Rachel Thomson (Ont.) | Government | Entire campaign | | | |
| Rita Ubriaco (Ont.) | Government | Entire campaign | | Yes | |
| W.J. Weir (Ont.) | Government | Entire campaign | | | |
| Jerry Herman (Man.–Sask.) | Government | 10 days | | | |
| John Ivanstryn (Man.–Sask.) | Government | Entire campaign | | | |
| Howard Leeson (Man.–Sask.) | Government | Entire campaign | | | |
| Paul J. Lewans (Man.–Sask.) | Government | Entire campaign | | | |

Table 1.3 (cont'd)
Summary of proposals to regulate polls during election periods

| Intervener | Type of intervention[a] | Restriction period | Survey specifications sheet[b] (s. 98.1, Bill C-79) | Exit polls | Election expenses[c] |
|---|---|---|---|---|---|
| A.J. Moreau (Man.–Sask.) | Government | Entire campaign | | | |
| Ted Murphy, Renald Guay (Man.–Sask.) | Government | 2 weeks | Yes | | |
| Ed Whelan (Man.–Sask.) | Government | Entire campaign | | | |
| A.J. Moddejonge (Alta.–NWT) | Laissez-faire | | | | |
| Margo Jean (BC–YT) | Government | 2 weeks | | | |
| Andrey Lasichuk (BC–YT) | Government | Entire campaign | | | |
| R.P. Macnaughton (BC–YT) | Government | Entire campaign | | | |
| Don Cameron (BC–YT) | Government | 14 days | Yes | | |
| David Crawford (BC–YT) | Laissez-faire | | | | |
| K.W. Rymer (BC–YT) | Government | Entire campaign | | | |

Source: Royal Commission on Electoral Reform and Party Financing, Research 1991.

Note: When no information is given on an issue, the intervener did not mention it.

[a]Here we attempted to identify as accurately as possible the type of intervention preferred by each intervener. However, in some cases interveners favoured regulation for one specific issue but were generally in favour of laissez-faire. This is the position taken by Angus Reid and the Association canadienne de la radio et de la télévision de langue française, among others, who favoured laissez-faire in general but recommended that exit polls be regulated and that a 48-hour blackout be put in place. Since such cases were relatively rare, we preferred to discuss them in the text.

[b]Interveners basically commented on the specifications sheet proposed in Bill C-79. Some, however, requested the addition of other methodological items. We preferred to group together the remarks and suggestions concerning the appropriateness of legislation requiring that polling organizations include certain technical information when they publish and broadcast their polls.

[c]This was a relatively marginal issue for interveners. However, we thought it important to include the matter, as it was a significant question raised by the Commissioners during the hearings.

Democratic Party) all favoured a laissez-faire approach to polls, their membership clearly remained divided on the subject. For example, the Progressive Conservative party came out against section 98.1(1) of Bill C-79, which would have required that all public opinion polls be accompanied by certain methodological information: the name and address of the person or organization that conducted the poll; the size of the sample; the period during which interviews were conducted; the name and address of the person or organization that paid for the poll; the margin of error; and the exact wording of the questions. However, five of the seven PC constituency associations that submitted briefs to the Commission favoured government regulation. One of these agreed with section 98.1(1), and only two endorsed the official position of their party. The former leader of the Progressive Conservative Party of Ontario even stated that he favours a complete ban on polls during election campaigns.

Opinions varied even more widely in the Liberal party. Only the national executive of the Liberal Party of Canada opposed section 98.1(1); at the same time, it suggested that polling expenditures be counted as election expenses. However, five provincial associations (Quebec, Alberta, British Columbia, Nova Scotia and Prince Edward Island) and five local associations stated publicly that they favoured some kind of regulation. Recommendations regarding the period during which the publication of election polls should be banned ranged from 72 hours prior to the election to the entire campaign. The latter position was supported by two associations. Included in this range were periods of 10 days, two weeks and four weeks, and as of mid-campaign. Four local and provincial associations, including that of Alberta, favoured the disclosure of polling methodologies.

As with the Liberal party, the national executive of the New Democratic Party, which also favoured laissez-faire, urged that expenditures involved in polling be included as election expenses. (It should be emphasized here that the Conservative party spent almost $5 million on polls during the 1988 federal election, whereas the Liberal party spent only $600 000 and the NDP spent only $300 000. These expenditures were not included as election expenses by the parties.) The NDP associations of Saskatchewan and Prince Edward Island, however, preferred government regulation, the former advocating publication of survey specifications and the latter recommending that polls be prohibited during the last two weeks of an election campaign. Two local associations favoured a ban on polls for the entire campaign.

Among the other political parties heard by the Commission, the Parti nationaliste du Québec and the Green Party of Canada from

Niagara Falls supported section 98.1 of Bill C-79. The Confederation of Regions Western Party recommended a complete prohibition of polls in election periods: consistent with its other proposals for fixed dates for elections, it felt the ban should apply to the 90 days preceding the vote. Only the Rhinoceros Party was in favour of laissez-faire.

Finally, of the seven past and present parliamentarians and candidates who appeared before the Commission, five advocated government regulation, one favoured laissez-faire, and one was undecided. Three interveners were in favour of having pollsters publish and broadcast their methodology standards, and one advocated the prohibition of polls during all election campaigns. A former MP from Winnipeg, although in favour of laissez-faire, stated that a short end-of-campaign "breather" was probably necessary. Lastly, Judy Whitaker, a former New Democratic Party candidate from Prince Edward Island, asked for government regulations banning both exit polls and the publication or broadcasting of such Canadian polls in the U.S. media.

Political parties and organizations constituted the majority of witnesses heard by the Commission on the subject of polling, submitting about 40 percent of the briefs on opinion polls. Twenty-nine of the 37 briefs recommended government regulation; 15 of these advocated a period of restriction during the campaign; 11 recommended publication of survey specifications; and one urged a prohibition on exit polls. Only two Liberal associations advocated that polls be prohibited and that methodological standards used for polls be published. Five interveners were in favour of some kind of government intervention but did not specify what kind.

The considerable differences between the positions taken by national party executives and those of their members are no doubt symptoms of the difficulty Canadian élites have communicating with the public. The party élite would no doubt respond that interveners at a Royal Commission are there mainly to promote their own points of view and not those held by the majority of members and that the other members probably agree with the executive, or they would be present. Nevertheless, there is no empirical evidence for that. Perhaps Canadian political parties should question this phenomenon – a phenomenon common to the three main political parties. An effort should be made to find more satisfactory answers.

### Journalists and Broadcasters

Only one group opposed any government regulation whatsoever, and that is the group that would be affected by such legislation: journalists and broadcasters. Five out of seven from this group supported laissez-faire, and two recommended self-regulation. Concealed by this unanimity, however, were various forms of regulation that seem somewhat incompatible with the very idea of status quo. The Quebec Federation of Professional Journalists (QFPJ), for example, while opposing section 98.1 of Bill C-79 because it represents a threat to freedom of the press, conceded that a 48-hour blackout prohibiting all publication or broadcasting of opinion polls before the vote would be an acceptable compromise and would respect every individual's right to have time to reply. The Federation was also in favour of banning exit polls. The Association canadienne de la radio et de la télévision de langue française adopted a similar position, although it had no comments with respect to the survey specifications sheet. Only VOCM-Radio of St. John's, Newfoundland, was in favour of laissez-faire and the publication of methodological information.

The QFPJ and the Canadian Broadcasting Corporation (CBC) were the only groups to come out in favour of self-regulation. The QFPJ emphasized that polling organizations, especially in Quebec, have their own codes of ethics and that the Comité des sondages of the Regroupement québécois des sciences sociales acts as a watchdog, helping to enforce standards. The CBC emphasized that it had developed a code of conduct to serve as a guide for journalists, as well as for the production and broadcasting of polls by this Crown corporation. The code prohibits the commissioning of polls by the CBC during the last 10 days of a campaign. In the case of the other broadcast media, we will no doubt have to rely on their sense of social responsibility.

### Pollsters and Researchers

Three polling firms were in favour of laissez-faire (Angus Reid, Environics, Gallup); one advocated self-regulation (Sorécom); and one recommended government regulation (Omnifacts Research). It is interesting to note that Angus Reid considered section 98.1(1) unfair, stating that this provision adds to existing pressure on those in charge of polling organizations, who also have to deal with competition and market forces. However, like Omnifacts Research, Angus Reid wished to see exit polls prohibited. Omnifacts not only supported government intervention but also wished to see a 24-hour blackout covering polling day, thus making exit polls impossible; this organization also recommended that survey specifications sheets be made public. Omnifacts was the only intervener recommending that a polling commission be established under the authority of the Chief Electoral Officer of Canada and that all organizations file their survey reports with this commission. It should also be noted that the "official" pollsters for the two main political parties, Decima Research and Goldfarb Consultants, were conspicuous by their absence during Commission hearings.

With respect to associations of university researchers, the Regroupement québécois des sciences sociales (RQSS), which was established in 1977 and includes members from both the Société québécoise de science politique and the Association canadienne des sociologues et anthropologues de langue française, favoured a certain amount of government regulation at all times, not just during elections. For example, the RQSS advocated the publication of a standard "methodology insert" by all Canadian media each time they publish a poll. This measure, although not guaranteeing that a given poll would meet all scientific standards governing the production of poll surveys, would at least ensure that polling results and data were accompanied by more technical information. In the opinion of the RQSS, such a step would not amount to dictating to the print media what information must accompany the publication or distribution of a poll, but rather to acknowledging that the public has the right to be fully informed.

The RQSS also recommended establishing a polling commission, whose main duty would be to ensure the accuracy and reliability of election polls published or broadcast by the media. All polling organizations would have to make available to the members of this commission all of the data, reports and other relevant information pertaining to the broadcasting or publication of polls. Members of the public could also have access to such data and could submit complaints to the commission if they felt their right to information was being denied. The RQSS did not suggest, however, under whose authority such a commission should fall.

Finally, among university researchers, Agar Adamson of Acadia University advocated self-regulation for the short term; Vincent Lemieux of Université Laval recommended laissez-faire; and five professors from western Canada recommended a prohibition on polls for the entire length of the election campaign. Thus, a diversity of opinion can be found even within the university community.

### Interest Groups and Individual Citizens

In all, 12 interest groups from various parts of the country expressed reservations about publishing and broadcasting polls during elections. Eight citizens' groups were in favour of regulation, and four favoured laissez-faire. Three chambers of commerce made statements on the subject: the Moncton Chamber of Commerce advocated that polls be prohibited as of mid-campaign; the Calgary Chamber of Commerce recommended stricter rules governing methodological standards; and the Thompson Chamber of Commerce came out in favour of laissez-faire. Three associations wished to see polls banned for the entire duration of the campaign, while three others wanted tighter rules on disclosure of survey specifications sheets. Only one association, Citizens Concerned about Free Trade, asked that exit polls be prohibited altogether.

The second largest group to submit briefs on the subject of polling, after political parties and associations, consisted of members of the general public; no fewer than 25 individual citizens (28 percent of interveners on the subject) made statements on the role of opinion polls during elections. Most of these statements, however, concerned the period during which opinion polls should be prohibited during election campaigns; 23 individuals favoured a ban on polls ranging from 10 days to the entire length of the campaign; only 2 opted for laissez-faire. In fact, 14 individuals recommended a total prohibition on polls during elections; 5 opted for a ban of two weeks; and 2 opted for a 10-day ban. Only 4 individuals advocated stricter standards of methodology, and 1 intervener recommended that exit polls be prohibited.

## CONCLUSION

Despite a flourishing debate on the role of polls in modern democratic societies, relatively few conclusions can be drawn. To date, theories about the decline of political parties and the undue influence of polls on voters have not been convincingly supported.[3] This also holds true for the briefs submitted to the Royal Commission; the actual effects of polls during election campaigns remain difficult to pinpoint. Although the executives of the large political parties are in favour of the status quo, party members and local organizations call for a stiffening of the standards governing survey methodology and closer supervision of surveys during elections.

In summary, an analysis of the 90 briefs submitted to the Commission shows the following:

- Political organizations submitted a total of 37 briefs; associations of journalists and broadcasters, 7; pollsters and researchers, 9; interest groups, 12; and ordinary citizens, 25.
- Sixty-three briefs favoured regulating polls during election periods (70.0 percent); 22 were in favour of laissez-faire (24.4 percent); 3 favoured self-regulation (3.3 percent); and 2 took no definitive position (0.3 percent).
- The executives of the three main Canadian political parties (Progressive Conservative, Liberal and New Democratic) were all in favour of laissez-faire.

- Five of seven Progressive Conservative riding associations, the 10 Liberal provincial riding associations and the four New Democratic associations favoured regulation.
- Of the 37 briefs submitted by political parties and organizations, 29 called for regulation, 15 for the restriction of polling during election periods, 11 for the publication of a specifications sheet and 1 for the banning of exit polls.
- Associations of broadcasters and journalists called for a laissez-faire approach in five of seven cases, while two favoured self-regulation; however, the QFPJ called for a 48-hour blackout, and the CBC already has its own code that prohibits the financing of polls during the final 10 days of a campaign.
- Polling organizations called for the preservation of laissez-faire in three of five cases, one favoured self-regulation, and one, regulation.
- University researchers called for regulation in two of four cases, laissez-faire in one case, and in another, self-regulation followed by regulation if self-regulation did not achieve the desired results.
- Eight interest groups favoured regulation and four, laissez-faire.
- Of the 25 citizens who submitted briefs to the Commission, 23 favoured the banning of polls for periods ranging from 10 days to the entire election campaign; 2 chose laissez-faire.

# 3

# CANADIAN
# LEGISLATION
# ON POLLING

~

THERE IS NO CANADIAN LAW specifically regulating the publication of polls during elections, though it has been suggested that some legislation with broader intentions might affect polling. For example, the 1968 *Broadcasting Act* (section 28(1)) prohibited the broadcasting of any partisan programming during the 48 hours before the close of polls in any election. There was speculation that the broadcasting or discussion of poll results during this period might constitute political broadcasting and fall under the prohibition. However, this interpretation was never tested. In fact, the blackout provision for federal elections was moved into the *Canada Elections Act* in 1974 and applied only to party and candidate advertising (sections 48 and 213). It was eventually dropped from the *Broadcasting Act*. Subsequently, the CRTC notified broadcasters that while section 28(1), later 19(1), still applied to referendums and provincial or municipal elections, it would be applied only to advertising and not to any form of broadcast journalism (Soderlund et al. 1984, 119–20). The section was dropped altogether in the major revisions that led to the 1991 *Broadcasting Act*.

The *Canada Elections Act* itself contains no specific provisions regarding polls but a number of attempts have been made over the past 20 years to amend the Act to deal with polls. However, any amendments would have to comply with the *Canadian Charter of Rights and Freedoms*, with its guarantees of freedom of expression, unless its provisions were overridden by the notwithstanding clause. In the absence of legal restrictions, the Charter has not been invoked in the case of polls but there have been cases that might be relevant to any measures to regulate published polls.

The applicability of existing laws to the publication of polls has been the subject of debate and confusion. For example, Alexandre Lazareff, in his interpretation of the blackout provision in the 1968

*Broadcasting Act,* states that Canada is one of the countries that have prohibited the broadcasting of polls dealing with the election during the final two days of the campaign (Lazareff 1984, 25).[4] This interpretation is repeated in Meynaud and Duclos (1985, 115). However, this view is unwarranted, as the broadcasting of poll results has never been determined to constitute political programming under the Act.

### THE *BROADCASTING ACT*

Most of the discussion of polling in the context of the *Broadcasting Act* has involved the blackout provision that prohibits political broadcasting during the final 48 hours of an election campaign. Section 28(1) of the 1968 Act reads as follows:

> No broadcaster shall broadcast, and no licensee of a broadcasting receiving undertaking shall receive a broadcast of a program, advertisement or announcement of a partisan character in relation to
>
> (*a*) a referendum, or
>
> (*b*) an election of a member of the House of Commons, the legislature of a province or the council of a municipal corporation
>
> that is being held or is to be held within the area normally served by the broadcasting undertaking of the broadcaster or such licensee, *on the day of any such referendum or election or on the one day immediately preceding the day of any such referendum or election.* [emphasis added]

The Act provided for a fine of up to $5 000 for any licensee found guilty of violating the blackout provisions.

The revised provisions in section 19(1) deleted reference to the House of Commons and permitted provinces to opt out of the blackout. In those cases where provinces did legislate in this area, however, they generally extended the blackout or specified more clearly what was covered, rather than opting out.

While election polls have not been the subject of any regulations under the Act, the reasoning in the two cases that have been decided in relation to this provision – that of Gordon Sinclair and Toronto radio station CFRB and that of CJON in St. John's, Newfoundland – might be relevant to any future attempts to regulate the broadcast of reports on election-related polls.

### The Sinclair Case

During the 1971 Ontario election campaign, in a news bulletin on the eve of the election, Gordon Sinclair, a Toronto broadcaster, made a partisan comment supporting incumbent Premier William Davis and vehemently condemning various sections of the *Broadcasting Act* that he felt were unfair and discriminatory. His remarks were as follows:

> The Ontario elections. With 4,400,000 potential voters to elect 117 members comes tomorrow and what should be good weather. The consensus of opinion from all 3 major parties – although 5 parties are taking part – is that the Conservatives under Bill Davis will win. Liberals say their Conservative opponents will have the most seats at 51, well balanced in the present figure of 67 and well short of the majority. The New Democratic Party says the Conservatives will have 58, one short of a majority. The Conservatives themselves say they will have 60 to 80. My own figure says Conservatives 62, Liberals 33, NDP 22. This, after selection of a speaker, would give the Davis government a majority of 6 and these figures are my own, based merely on hunches. An important set of if's concerns the way the youth vote will go. The 17 Conservative resignations headed by John Robarts and the potential disillusionment over regional government. Perhaps the Spadina Expressway and the Roman Catholic school issue will play an important part. These affairs show Davis to be a man of decision. Surely an asset in any leader.
>
> There is a stupid rule which says that newspapers are free to comment in this way – the way I am doing now – but radio stations and their people like me are supposed to remain silent. We're to be silent 48 hours before the elections. Well, I am not silent and I am saying I am not silent. And I am not just making a mistake, I am defying this stupid rule. I think the rule is absolutely nuts. It is discriminatory in favour of newspapers. And it's an insult to voters' intelligence. So let's see if me, Gordon Sinclair, is paraded on the carpet for expressing my views about the way my province should be run on the eve of an election. So, I am here at CFRB and my name is Gordon Sinclair and I am saying what I think.

After one court had dismissed the application of the Toronto station, claiming it had no jurisdiction in this area (*CFRB* (No. 1) 1973), the case and the debate surrounding it were taken before a higher court. In October 1972 (*CFRB* (No. 2) 1973), the Ontario High Court of Justice dismissed CFRB's application to have section 28 acknowledged as being ultra vires (outside the power of) Parliament and in contravention of the *Canadian Bill of Rights* because it restricts the intellectual content of broadcasts. The court also stated that the Parliament of Canada has exclusive jurisdiction over radio communication (*Reference re Regulation and Control of Radio Communication* 1932). In its judgement, the court stated that, even though the conduct of provincial elections is a provincial matter, federal legislation may indirectly affect matters under provincial jurisdiction. The court also emphasized that the sole purpose of restraining broadcasters from making partisan comments is to allow any person or political party that might be harmed by such comments the time to reply.

The judgement, while acknowledging that the Act places newspapers and other information media in different categories, stated that this does not contravene the *Canadian Bill of Rights* and that the provisions of the section in no way restrict broadcasters' freedom of speech. The *Bill of Rights* did not, of course, have the constitutional status of the Charter.

The case was taken to the Ontario Court of Appeal, which on 21 June 1973 upheld the decision of the lower court (*CFRB* (C.A.) 1973). The decision of the Court of Appeal was that the section is intra vires (within the power of) Parliament. The federal government, said the court, is entitled to legislate in this area even if the legislation applies to provincial elections as well; the fact that the Act also concerns provincial elections does not constitute sufficient grounds to deny the meaning of the Act.

Furthermore, the judgement indicated clearly that it is the responsibility of Parliament to safeguard the public interest and to ensure that voters' choices during a democratic election are not influenced by media abuses. The judgement emphasized protection of the right of citizens to express their views freely on subjects of public concern and that any erosion of their political independence must be resisted. It also emphasized that a primary objective of electoral regulations is to ensure that voters are not subjected to undue influence.

Thus, the judgement affirmed that limiting partisan broadcasts for 48 hours at the end of an election campaign does not constitute an undue restriction because the prohibition is intended to allow time for partisan statements to be rebutted before the vote. The section is part of a code of conduct during elections in Canada that seeks to prevent broadcasters from abusing the principle of free expression. The case was later appealed to the Supreme Court of Canada, but it was dismissed on 13 November 1973.

On 29 March 1974, the Toronto radio station was ordered to pay a fine of $5 000 (*R. v. CFRB Ltd.* 1976).[5] In his judgement, the Honourable Mr. Justice A.W. Davidson examined the partisan nature of Sinclair's commentary and stated that by backing Premier Davis, the journalist had shown support for a specific candidate and political party.

Furthermore, he said, a broadcast may be partisan in nature even if it is not endorsed by a candidate or political party. The radio station subsequently took the case to the Ontario Court of Appeal on a question of law concerning the definition of "partisan." Although the appeal was dismissed on this point, the Honourable Mr. Justice J.A. Arnup defined any partisan broadcast as one intended to favour one election candidate over another or one referendum point of view over another. Thus, the message that is broadcast need not have a political sponsor.

### The CJON-TV Case

This case was brought before the courts following a by-election in St. John's, Newfoundland, in 1979. The case (*Mahoney* 1981) dealt with a political advertisement broadcast on 24 September 1979, the day before the by-election. The CRTC instituted proceedings against the Newfoundland Broadcasting Company Ltd. (CJON-TV in St. John's) for contravening the blackout section of the *Broadcasting Act*. The broadcaster argued that the section was ultra vires because it represented a delegation of power in broadcasting matters to the provinces and that the federal government cannot legislate in areas of provincial jurisdiction. In its decision, rendered on 5 December 1980, the court stated that the purpose of the section was not to delegate power over broadcasting to the provinces, but rather to encourage uniform rules for elections (with provinces permitted to opt out).

Lastly, the court dealt with the question of whether the case involved strict or absolute responsibility – that is, whether the radio station deliberately broke the law. The court concluded that the radio station either had to have been aware of section 28(1) or could easily have found out. CJON-TV's offence was one of absolute responsibility: the court determined that the company had not taken all necessary measures to ensure compliance and was therefore liable.

## PROVINCIAL LEGISLATION ON BROADCASTING AND THE REGULATION OF POLLS

The first legislation in Canada (and the only provincial legislation) to attempt to regulate polls was that passed by the British Columbia legislature in 1939. The Act in question was aimed especially at regulating polls:

> 166. No person, corporation or organization shall, after the issue of the writ for any election, take any straw vote which will, prior to the election, distinguish the political opinions of the voters in any electoral district. (British Columbia *Election Act*, R.S.B.C. 1979, c. 103, s. 166)

In 1982, British Columbia repealed this provision (British Columbia *Election Amendment Act*, S.B.C. 1982, c. 48, s. 29).

The blackout provision of the federal legislation, which is concerned with partisan broadcasts in the days preceding the vote, was included by New Brunswick and Alberta in their own electoral laws.

Thus, in 1973, New Brunswick included in its *Elections Act* the following provision prohibiting any person from broadcasting any type of partisan message on radio or television just prior to the vote:

> 117(3) No person shall, on the ordinary polling day or on either of the two days immediately preceding it, broadcast over any radio or television station,
>
> (*a*) a speech,
>
> (*b*) any entertainment, or
>
> (*c*) any advertising program
>
> in favour of or on behalf of any political party or any candidate. (New Brunswick *Elections Act*, R.S.N.B. 1973, c. E-3)

What is unique about the New Brunswick law is that the subsequent article stipulates that any individual using a radio or television station *outside* the province is also guilty of an illegal practice:

> 117(4) Any person who uses, aids, abets, counsels or procures the use of any radio or television station outside New Brunswick during the period mentioned in subsection (3) for the broadcasting of any matter having reference to the election is guilty of an illegal practice. (New Brunswick *Elections Act*, R.S.N.B. 1973, c. E-3)

A maximum fine of $500 for any such improper practice is provided for in section 118(2).

In 1980, Alberta also passed legislation designed to regulate the broadcasting of partisan messages in accordance with the federal *Broadcasting Act*. Legislators in that province were more specific in their intentions, however, indicating clearly in the *Elections Act* that any party advertising would be prohibited for the 48 hours preceding the election. Section 129 reads as follows:

> No political party, registered political party, candidate or official agent or any other person may advertise on the facilities of any broadcasting undertaking as defined in section 2 of the *Broadcasting Act* (Canada)

(a) on polling day, or

(b) on the day immediately preceding polling day,

for the purpose of promoting or opposing a particular political party, registered political party, or the election of a particular candidate. (Alberta *Elections Act*, R.S.A. 1980, c. E-2, s. 129)

To the extent to which these provisions regulate broadcasters, they may be challenged, now that the blackout section is no longer a part of the *Broadcasting Act,* since jurisdiction over broadcasting is exclusively federal. However, it seems clear that the provinces can regulate the conduct of their citizens in respect to provincial and municipal elections, as long as no Charter rights are violated. The capacity of provincial election laws to regulate the broadcasting of poll reports is unclear.

## ELECTION ACTS: PROPOSALS FOR REGULATING POLLS
At present, no specific provisions covering polling are contained in either federal or provincial legislation. Over the years, however, several attempts have been made by both levels of government to include provisions governing pre-election polls. Unfortunately, all such efforts have been unsuccessful. However, consensus about the need for such regulation, especially among MPs, is growing because of the increasingly significant role that polls play in election campaigns.

### Federal Efforts
The *Canada Elections Act* contains no specific provisions regulating polls. This can be explained, in part, by the fact that the Act has not been significantly amended since 1974; the increased role played by opinion polls in election campaigns dates from about the same time. The first proposal to prohibit the publication of pre-election polls in Canada came in 1966, when the Committee on Election Expenses, chaired by Alphonse Barbeau, recommended a total prohibition on polls for the entire length of election campaigns (Canada, Committee 1966, 51). This proposal was never implemented.

Subsequently, according to Magnant's (1980) study of bills tabled in the House of Commons between 1970 and 1980, no fewer than 22 such bills were submitted. Among the most noteworthy were private members' bills proposed by Robert Coates (Bill C-213; first reading, 15 October 1974) and John Reynolds (Bill C-404; first reading, 10 July 1975), both aimed at prohibiting the publication of polls at election time. The Standing Committee on Privileges and Elections studied the two bills but rejected them both (Canada, House of Commons 1976).

Similar proposals, in particular those of Arnold Peters and Adrien Lambert (19 December 1978) and Hal Herbert (Bill C-319, 30 October 1978), met with the same fate. Other bills, among them those of Dean Whiteway (Bill C-455, 15 May 1978; Bill C-459, 7 June 1978; Bill C-265, 30 October 1978), aimed not so much at banning polls during elections as at providing guidelines for their publication and broadcasting: these bills proposed that polls be accompanied by information on methodology.

In June 1980, a major debate took place in the House of Commons between those who wished to see polls prohibited during election campaigns and those opposed to any regulation. The main argument supporting the laissez-faire approach was that there is no need for the government to define what is accurate or inaccurate in the media and that any action limiting access to information could constitute a dangerous precedent. Those who advocated a total or partial ban maintained that polls tend to discourage people from voting and at the same time transform parliamentary democracy into direct democracy.

An even more important debate, held between 9 and 17 October 1980, was on the confidentiality of polls conducted for the federal government during the pre-referendum period. Between January 1979 and the autumn of 1980, the federal government conducted an estimated 141 polls, at a total cost of $5 million. The issue raised by the debate was whether the publication of such polls at election time contravenes democratic principles, especially if a government uses them for partisan purposes and invokes national security to avoid disclosing information on methodology. In our opinion, the bureaucracy uses the confidentiality of surveys as a cloak to hide intentions that run counter to the principle of accountability.

In June 1987, the president of the Privy Council presented Bill C-79 in the House of Commons. The bill included several amendments to the *Canada Elections Act*, among them a section on opinion polls. Section 98.1 was similar to many of the proposals that went before it. It was designed to require the print and electronic media to accompany the publication or broadcasting of any poll with specified information concerning methodology. The section read as follows:

> 98.1(1) The results of every commissioned opinion poll in relation to a candidate or registered party that are printed or broadcast by printed or electronic media must, in each printing or at the time of the broadcast, be accompanied by the disclosure of
>
> (a) the name and address of the person or organization that conducted the inquiry;

(b)  the size of the sample;

(c)  the dates of the first and last completed interviews;

(d)  the name and address of the person or organization who paid for the conduct of the opinion poll;

(e)  the margin of error if calculable; and

(f)  the exact wording of each question the answers to which led to the results so printed or broadcast.

Bill C-79 also provided for prosecution in the event of any violation of these provisions:

> 98.1(2) Every person who prints or broadcasts or who causes to be printed or broadcast, by printed or broadcast media the results of any opinion poll referred to in subsection (1) without the disclosures referred to in that subsection is guilty of an offence and is liable on summary conviction
>
> (a)  in the case of an individual, to a fine not exceeding five thousand dollars; and
>
> (b)  in the case of a corporation, to a fine not exceeding twenty-five thousand dollars.

It should be noted that Bill C-79 would have made the chief electoral officer (CEO) responsible for enforcing these provisions; any complaint about them would be brought to the CEO's attention, as is the case for other complaints under the *Canada Elections Act*.

Like the other proposals for regulating pre-election polls, Bill C-79 died on the order paper when the 33rd Parliament was dissolved: the members had not been able to agree on the issue of election expenses, another aspect of the bill. The CEO at the time, Jean-Marc Hamel, suggested in his 1989 report that the bill be split up, so that the uncontentious sections – among which he counted the section on opinion polls – could be adopted quickly (Canada, Chief Electoral Officer 1989, 44).

## Provincial Efforts

The Ontario legislature also heard several proposals to regulate polls during elections. Noteworthy here are those bills filed by George Samis, who proposed that polls be prohibited during elections (Bill 165, 22 November 1976; Bill 29, 28 June 1977). In April 1978, the Ontario legislature debated George Ashe's motion recommending that the house consider adopting legislation prohibiting the publication of election polls. The Liberals and the NDP supported the proposal; the Progressive Conservatives did not pursue the debate (Ontario 1978, 1966–67). In May 1979, the provincial Minister of Justice and Deputy Premier stated that "the government is giving consideration to drafting legislation in the spirit of [Ashe's] resolution, although no definite decision has yet been taken" (Ontario 1979, 1416). Still awaiting the Minister's decision, the leader of the Progressive Conservatives introduced a bill limiting the publication of election polls (Ontario 1979, 1677, Bill 79). There are still no regulations in place in Ontario.

In Quebec, the Parti québécois is the only party to have included a ban on the publication of polls during the last week of a campaign in its party platform; this it did in the early 1970s. Certain government initiatives were also taken. After the 30 April 1979 by-election in the riding of Jean-Talon, MNA Fernand Grenier of the Union nationale requested that the government table a bill to regulate polls. In his speech before the National Assembly, Grenier emphasized the fact that a survey had placed the Liberals and the Parti québécois nose-to-nose in this by-election. However, the results were entirely different. The Liberal party walked away with 57.7 percent of the votes in the riding of Jean-Talon, versus 35.3 percent (Quebec 1979–80, 1032–33).

Furthermore, in 1979, the polling committee of the Regroupement québécois des sciences sociales submitted a brief to the Minister of State for Electoral and Parliamentary Reform containing several proposals to improve the use of polls by journalists and to encourage increased accessibility to poll results broadcast during referendum campaigns (Comité des sondages 1979). In the specific context of the pre-referendum period, Quebec academics were concerned that with so many polls being conducted the public would not be able to distinguish between "good" and "poor" polls in the heat of the moment and that certain minimum standards of polling would lose out to partisan considerations. The committee's recommendations can be summarized as follows:

1. The results of opinion polls that have been published or broadcast, both in their original form and in any other form they may subsequently take, should be accompanied by certain information on methodology (name of sponsor, population studied, interview period, average length of interviews, type of sample, number of questionnaires completed, response rate).

2. All opinion polls, as well as documents pertaining to their production, should be deposited legally, on the day of their broadcast or publication at the latest, with a recognized organization (e.g.,

National Library, Bibliothèque de l'Assemblée nationale, office of the chief electoral officer, the courts).

3. The publication and broadcasting of opinion polls should be prohibited during the week prior to the election; public discussion on published surveys, however, would still be allowed.

Once again, these proposals did not give rise to legislation.

More recently, on 9 June 1983, Liberal MNA Richard French proposed a 32-section bill aimed at regulating polls and government advertising (Quebec 1983–84, 2072). Although differing in scope from other proposals (its main objective was to regulate government polls), this bill constitutes an interesting attempt to have governments establish strict rules on polling within the bureaucracy and at the same time make such polls available to the public. French's bill died on the order paper. He reintroduced the bill on 15 May 1985, but it met the same fate (Quebec 1984–85, 3550).

To our knowledge, the only other province to tackle the issue of banning pre-election polls is Nova Scotia. On 27 January 1961, Nova Scotia's Royal Commission on Provincial Elections proposed that its *Election Act* include a provision banning the publication of straw polls. The government did not follow up on the matter, however, believing that it would be quite difficult to establish mechanisms to control this type of poll (Canada, House of Commons 1976, 38:28).

## POLLS AND THE CHARTER

One of the main objectives of Bill C-79 was to make the *Canada Elections Act* consistent with the *Canadian Charter of Rights and Freedoms*. On the issue of opinion polls, there were two questions that would need interpreting in light of the Charter: Would restricting the publication or broadcast of election polls during elections contravene the spirit of the Charter? Would compelling the media to publish or broadcast their methodology standards violate freedom of the press?

In his 1989 report, the Chief Electoral Officer of Canada, Jean-Marc Hamel, pointed out that the 1982 adoption of the Charter and its inclusion in the Constitution had prompted debate about the application of the Charter to election matters. Hamel emphasized, among other points, that the 1988 federal election was the first real test of the Charter and that, in fact, a significant number of cases contesting the *Canada Elections Act* had been based on the Charter. Hamel went on to say that "the 34th General Election may very well be looked back on as the 'Charter of Rights and Freedoms Election'" (Canada, Chief Electoral Officer 1989, 44).

As we have seen, there are still no specific provisions regulating opinion polls. However, certain court decisions pertaining to the *Broadcasting Act*, in particular those concerning the prohibition of partisan advertising 48 hours prior to an election, might have taken a different turn if the offences had been interpreted in light of the Charter, especially if we consider polls as a type of partisan information that could benefit a specific party or candidate.

## Air Time

The judgement of the Ontario Court of Appeal in the Gordon Sinclair case provides a basis for arguing that a ban on partisan advertising for a certain length of time does not contravene the Charter. As it was decided before the Charter, however, the ruling is not definitive. These cases do, however, underscore the fact that a balance must be struck between freedom of expression and the need for a system of rules to ensure fairness in electoral competition. The courts viewed the 48-hour blackout as a reasonable part of a code of conduct established by Parliament for election campaigns. Under the Charter, they might well do so again. However, the blackout rule might well be challenged and there is precedent in the United States for regarding the rule as unconstitutional (*Mills* 1966).

## Partisan Advertising

In their analysis of Canadian law concerning the broadcasting of partisan advertising, Kathleen Mahoney and Sheilah L. Martin (1985, 3.18–3.23) state that legislators have restricted freedom of expression to limit broadcasting during elections on the basis of two principles: fairness and social responsibility. Fairness involves the right of the public and political candidates to respond to any information that could be prejudicial to them. Section 1382 of the *Civil Code*, regarding civil liability (which, of course, applies only in Quebec), provides that anyone whose actions result in harm to another person is responsible for taking the proper corrective measures (*Civil Code*, chap. II, s. 1382, 236).

With respect to partisan advertising, the *Canada Elections Act* makes a distinction between registered political parties and candidates and other citizens. The Act requires broadcasters to make available both paid and (for networks) free time to registered parties. In addition, it establishes rules of equitable treatment for candidates. The guidelines and regulations of the Canadian Radio-television and Telecommunications Commission (CRTC) contain similar provisions. The potential conflict between freedom of expression and the rules necessary for fairness among those contesting an election was recognized early in the development of broadcast regulation (see, for example, the Board of

Broadcast Governors' white paper on political broadcasting (BBG 1961)). However, the CRTC has consistently maintained that it is up to broadcasters to ensure that the principles of fairness and of impartial, balanced information are respected (CRTC 1968).

In 1983, however, amendments to the *Canada Elections Act*, which were designed to protect the system of regulated competition established in the 1974 reforms, had the effect of awarding registered political parties and candidates a monopoly over certain kinds of campaign discourse. These provisions included a prohibition on anyone other than registered parties from incurring election expenses (section 70.1(1)) and restricted the printing, distribution and posting of election literature to registered parties and candidates (section 72). These provisions were challenged in an Alberta court by the National Citizens' Coalition in 1984 as a violation of the guarantee of freedom of expression in the *Canadian Charter of Rights and Freedoms* (section 2(*b*)). The Alberta Court of Queen's Bench agreed; as Beckton (1989, 222) observes, the judgement emphasized that freedom of expression is a basic democratic principle, especially at election time, and that these sections of the Act restrict that freedom.

Mr. Justice Medhurst rejected the Crown's arguments that these provisions of the *Canada Elections Act* were aimed solely at ensuring greater fairness among parties and candidates and that the absence of rules and a ceiling on advertising expenses might give individuals or interest groups with greater financial resources an unfair advantage. As Mahoney and Martin (1985, 3.21) point out, however, the Court's decision did not take into account how the doctrine of fairness applies to broadcasting or how the absence of government regulation can work against freedom of expression.

Since these sections of the *Canada Elections Act* were declared void and the Alberta judgement was not appealed, any group or individual may incur election expenses or purchase air time to support or oppose a party, candidate or policy. However, the issues that led to the 1983 amendments remain. In particular, a party or candidate – restricted by expenditure limits and advertising blackout rules – could be overwhelmed by an independent campaign funded by groups unfettered by those restrictions. A recent judgement by the Federal Court of Appeal (*Reference re N.B. Broadcasting Co. Ltd. and the CRTC* (1985)) held that section 2 of the Charter as applied to broadcasting gives no right to anyone to use radio frequencies, which are regulated under the *Broadcasting Act*. According to Mahoney and Martin (1985), it is therefore unlikely that the principle of fairness in broadcasting will disappear, because it is in the public interest. The problem is to find a balance between the requirements of fairness and of freedom of expression.

## The Obligation to Publish Information on Methodology

The main controversy surrounding the broadcasting or publication of pre-election polls has to do with the Bill C-79 provisions that would have compelled the media to make public certain information on polling methods. For many, in particular the British Columbia Civil Liberties Association, this type of provision contravenes section 2 of the Charter, which guarantees freedom of the press. The opinion of this association, like that of the Quebec Federation of Professional Journalists, was based on the principle that compelling the media to disclose such information could set a dangerous precedent that could open the door to abuses and jeopardize freedom of the press.

From this limited perspective, the argument certainly holds water; the courts, however, have examined the bigger picture, attempting to resolve the conflict between freedom of the press and the public's right to information. In legal terms, this means applying the "balancing test" to the debate, that is, comparing the arguments championed by various groups. The basic issue, which unfortunately has not been raised, is whether providing partial or erroneous information constitutes an affront to freedom of expression and the right to information. In such situations, should the freedom of certain groups, such as journalists, be restricted by imposing standards of conduct?

A major study by Professor Howard Kushner of the Faculty of Law at the University of British Columbia suggests new parameters for Canadian legislation on pre-election polls. Kushner (1983) examined both the constitutional validity of federal government action in this area and its implications under the Charter. Based on his analysis of case law, Kushner says that the main factor involved is the misuse of freedom of speech, which could lead, as in the Gordon Sinclair case, to the broadcasting of partisan messages. According to Kushner, however, a complete prohibition on the publication of polls during elections would be possible only if the government could show that polls affect the integrity of elections and influence the outcome. In Kushner's opinion, such a demonstration would be difficult, especially if the aim was to prohibit the conduct and publication of polls during elections; this would run counter to the principle that there should be no restrictions on access to new sources of ideas.

Kushner also acknowledges, however, that if the principle of the balancing test (as mentioned in several judgements) is accepted, legislators could enact regulations designed to allow the public to improve its understanding of polls and to assess their quality. Kushner does not see this type of regulation as having any effect on freedom of expression, especially if it does not influence the content of the information in question:

A "balancing test" requires an identification of the various interests involved. The reasons for restricting election polls must therefore be clearly articulated. If the basis for controls is the alleged inaccuracy of polls, then the legislation should attempt to ensure their accuracy through the stipulation of certain standards ... The pollsters have themselves adopted standards for this purpose. The disclosure of certain information, for example, the sampling method adopted, the sample size, those surveyed, and the wording of the question may result in more accurate surveys. Such legislation would be narrow in its operation, unconcerned with the content of the information. It would not therefore substantially impair the use of polls and would balance the interests concerned by permitting public access to this kind of information while ensuring a sufficient degree of accuracy. (Kushner 1983, 546)

Kushner (1983, 548) notes that if this method is adopted, the courts will also have to consider whether the legislation can be implemented within certain "reasonable limits," in other words, whether the regulatory means employed are excessively restrictive: "If the legislation merely stipulates disclosure requirements, and is not so onerous as to effectively eliminate polls, then it would appear to be reasonable. In fact the pollsters have voluntarily begun to adopt such standards."

As we will see in a later section of this study, researchers, pollsters, journalists and broadcasters have already adopted various codes of conduct with respect to polling both during and outside election periods; any legislation in this area would serve only to reinforce what already exists.

### The Quebec Charter of Rights and Freedoms

The various proposals put forward by the polling committee of the Regroupement québécois des sciences sociales were analysed by the Commission des droits de la personne du Québec in the light of Quebec's charter of rights and freedoms (Commission des droits de la personne du Québec 1979). As we will see, the human rights commission of Quebec dismissed the arguments of the British Columbia Civil Liberties Association, as well as those of the Quebec Federation of Professional Journalists.

According to the human rights commission of Quebec, three basic corollaries affect the public's right to be fully informed, and these must be respected in the context of an election or referendum campaign:

1. the availability of accessible, unrestricted information;

2. access to plentiful, diversified information; and
3. access to accurate, high-quality information, which implicitly guarantees the freedom to criticize that information.

Given these requirements, the human rights commission of Quebec drew the following conclusion: "Any regulation on opinion poll surveys that would tend to promote these corollaries, or conditions of practice, not only would not contravene Quebec's charter of human rights and freedoms, but could even be considered as contributing to the recognition and exercise of the right to information as defined in section 44" (Commission des droits de la personne du Québec 1979, 2).

The human rights commission of Quebec acknowledged the merits of proposals that opinion polls be accompanied by specific information on methodology and that polling organizations legally deposit all data and documents related to the production of a poll; the commission also approved in principle the terms and conditions involved. It also stated that any regulation of these two aspects of the polling process (compliance with methodological standards and public access to survey data) would promote the recognition and exercise of the right to information. At the same time, however, the commission expressed serious reservations: the requirement for legal deposit of all data and documents might interfere with the right to privacy (as stipulated in section 5 of the Charter) if access to polling data made it possible to identify and trace individual respondents. Accordingly, the commission proposed the use of "scrambling" techniques to ensure that no respondent could be identified.

With respect to the polling committee's third proposal – to prohibit the broadcasting or publication of any new polls during the week prior to the vote – the human rights commission of Quebec also expressed reservations and urged public debate on the issue, but decided against taking a position. The reasons for the commission's indecision were that although such a prohibition would interfere with freedom of expression, it might also encourage public debate and afford voters a better opportunity to consider the real issues at stake. The commission also emphasized that in a system with no restrictions, it would be impossible to correct any erroneous information published or broadcast during the final hours of a campaign. In short, this proposal would restrict the right to information, as defined in the commission's first two principles, in order to promote the third.

## CONCLUSION

A close reading of Canadian broadcasting law shows that, contrary to popular belief, there is nothing to prohibit the publication of opinion polls during the 48 hours prior to an election. Case law has not established that opinion polls constitute partisan information. In addition, the various efforts to restrict the broadcasting or publication of pre-election polls serve only to highlight the fact that no such rules exist in Canada. For example, as we will see, several polls were broadcast on the eve of the 1988 federal election.

We should also recall New Brunswick's rather remarkable election legislation, which prohibits the broadcasting of a partisan message from a transmitter located in a bordering province or country. This provision means that New Brunswick considers it illegal for a broadcaster in another province or the United States to broadcast any poll issued by a political party, organization or candidate pertaining to New Brunswick elections. In the case of legislation to prohibit the broadcasting or publication of opinion polls for a specified period of time, such a provision would no doubt be appropriate.

The *Canada Elections Act* does not deal explicitly with polling; at present, despite repeated attempts, the Act contains no provisions to ban the publication or broadcasting of pre-election polls. Recent proposals, in particular one made in June 1987, deal only with one aspect of regulation: the quality control of polls broadcast or published by the media. Most of the proposals, however, are aimed only at regulating polls published or broadcast during election campaigns; outside these periods, the proposed rules would not apply. In short, the publication or broadcasting of survey specifications sheets and other information on polling methodology remains of concern to legislators; however, the merits of applying such rules only during elections should be examined.

Furthermore, the notion of polls commissioned "in relation to a candidate or registered party," as stipulated in Bill C-79, seems to open the door to ambiguity concerning, in particular, polls on government policies. Under the C-79 scheme, no information on methodology would have to accompany a poll on a government's free trade policy, for example, as the poll would not be "in relation to a candidate or registered party." If legislators want to advance the public's right to accurate information, the legislation should apply to all types of polls. The French experience in this regard, as we will see, is instructive.

As well, it is very important to make a distinction between publishing and conducting a poll. Until now, efforts made by lawmakers have been aimed primarily at better monitoring the publication and release of pre-electoral polls, without infringing on any of the rights of the individual to conduct polls or to create polling organizations. Limitations on the release or publication of polls during election periods raise another important issue: Can a democratic society tolerate a situation where only some individuals have exclusive access to certain information? As well, an effective ban of the broadcasting or publication of polls would be difficult without the broadcasters, publishers and the parties themselves enforcing the applicable rules.

Last but not least, there is the issue of applying the *Canadian Charter of Rights and Freedoms*. Some hold the opinion that compelling polling organizations and the mass media to make public information on methodology does not interfere with freedom of speech; on the contrary, the lack of such information would seem to interfere with the public's right to know. Banning publication and broadcast of opinion polls during elections raises a number of questions, both legal and constitutional. Thus, the federal government would have to demonstrate how the broadcasting or publication of opinion polls affects the democratic process during an election campaign. Such an argument would be difficult to make before the courts, especially under the *Canadian Charter of Rights and Freedoms*.

# 4

# OPINION POLLS
## A Comparative Study
## of Legislation

~

IN THE PAST several years, a number of countries have passed laws to regulate the publication of pre-election polls: France, Malta, Portugal, Spain, Brazil, Venezuela and South Africa (which prohibits polls during the last 40 days of an election campaign) are some examples (Hoy 1989, 219–20). The use of polls as a means of information during pre-election periods remains extremely limited, as few countries have polling organizations capable of designing and conducting election polls. In addition, polling is not a common election practice in all countries, and many people still consider polls an intrusion that could interfere with the secrecy of the vote.

Our analysis deals mainly with countries that have attempted to regulate polling. This list is not exhaustive, for debates are still occurring in all countries where polling has become widespread, especially the industrialized ones. Our objective here is to outline the procedures followed by various governments and organizations in regulating polls and especially to identify the reasons that led legislators to adopt the chosen approach. We gathered information from many countries with and without polling regulations on the use of polling during and outside election periods.

In this chapter, we summarize efforts by the most representative countries to determine whether there are lessons for Canada. Over the years, and especially in the light of the U.S. experience with polling, several countries have adopted laws to regulate opinion polls during election campaigns. We begin our analysis with the United States, in particular the state of New York, which has passed a law to govern polling. We then examine how the European Community has tried to harmonize the laws of its member states, and we analyse the legislation of some of those countries in greater detail. Finally, we study some other noteworthy cases from the past few years and then take a closer look at a new polling technique – exit polling – that has remained relatively untouched by legislators.

## THE UNITED STATES

The first U.S. attempt to restrict the publication of polls during elections dates back to the failure of the *Literary Digest* poll in 1936. At the time, Senator Walter M. Pierce suggested that the publication of extrapolated polling results be prohibited during elections because it interfered with the normal electoral process (Stoetzel and Girard 1973, 51). In 1943, Senator Gerald Nye of North Dakota introduced a bill to oblige polling organizations to disclose sample size and to keep all documents pertaining to the production of any poll for a two-year period. These efforts produced no legislation.

It was not until May 1968 that another attempt to enact polling legislation was made. Lucien Nedzi, a member of Congress from Michigan, proposed that polling organizations deposit with the Library of Congress all information related to the production of any poll within 72 hours of its publication, in particular the sponsor's name and the poll methodology (Lazareff 1984, 26). Once again, however, Congress took no action.

### New York State

Among the American states, New York has adopted one of the most interesting approaches to polling legislation. Since 28 April 1978 New York has required all candidates and political organizations that quote poll results to provide information on the methods used. New York's law is unique because it specifies that candidates must not disclose the results of internal polls unless the public has access to the data in question. If such legislation were in force in Canada, candidates and political parties would not be permitted to refer to data from their own polls without disclosing the relevant information on methodology. The New York legislation clearly states that all such information must be made public within 48 hours of the disclosure of a poll, as must a statement of expenditures.

Section 3 of the New York legislation authorizes the State Board of Elections to issue opinions concerning the interpretation of the Act:

6201.2 Use of Public Opinion Polls
No candidate, political party or committee shall attempt to promote the success or defeat of a candidate by directly or indirectly disclosing or causing to be disclosed the results of a poll relating to a candidate for such an office or position, unless within 48 hours after such disclo-

sure, they provide the following information concerning the poll to the board or officer with whom statements or copies of statements of campaign receipts and expenditures are required to be filed by the candidate to whom such poll relates:

(a) The name of the person, party or organization that contracted for or who commissioned the poll and/or paid for it.

(b) The name and address of the organization that conducted the poll.

(c) The numerical size of the total poll sample, the geographic area covered by the poll and any special characteristics of the population included in the poll sample.

(d) The exact wording of the questions asked in the poll and the sequence of such questions.

(e) The method of polling – whether by personal interview, telephone, mail or other.

(f) The time period during which the poll was conducted.

(g) The number of persons in the poll sample: the number contacted who responded to each specific poll question; the number of persons contacted who did not so respond.

(h) The results of the poll. (New York, *Fair Campaign Code*, §6201.2)

In May 1984, the Board responded to a series of questions on the use of opinion polls by candidates during an election. The Board emphasized that because there is no federal legislation regulating opinion polls, the state law applies to all elections, including federal elections, held within New York's boundaries. The Board also stated that the law applies to polls conducted by designated candidates before their nomination, especially if they use polls to promote their candidacy or conduct themselves like the designated candidates; each case, however, must be evaluated on its own merits. Furthermore, the law applies to polls sponsored by individuals and organizations other than the candidate, including political parties and political action committees (PACs).

Moreover, in the opinion of the Board of Elections, the law requires candidates to reveal the results only of those poll questions made public and the order of these questions in the questionnaire, as well as all sample characteristics. Polls conducted by a political party or organization and made public for any reason, including unauthorized leaks or political "spying," must also be filed with the Board of Elections.

The Board of Elections has two major responsibilities: ensuring that the rules established under the *Fair Campaign Code* are respected and that candidates do not use polls to partisan ends; and ensuring that certain technical information always accompanies polling data filed with the Board.

Monitoring comments made by candidates during elections is not a uniquely U.S. problem. François Gazier, chair of the French polling commission, emphasized after the 1988 presidential election how difficult it is for a public organization to pinpoint what he calls pseudo- or crypto-polls. He mentioned, among others, certain cases in Marseille where the "commission had found the press and politicians on the radio referring to poll results, complete with figures, of which the commission had no knowledge and despite its efforts could not identify" (Gazier and de Leusse 1988, 5). Gazier believes that in certain cases inaccurate polls were involved. Like our U.S. respondents, however, he stressed the difficulties in monitoring this type of behaviour and verifying the validity of statements made. The same problem exists in Canada.

## MEMBERS OF THE EUROPEAN COMMUNITY: A COMPARISON

On 20 September 1976, the European Community adopted legislation to regulate European elections. This legislation established principles and guidelines on the coordination of dates and balloting in the member states, the counting of votes, universal direct suffrage, a five-year mandate for representatives, the differing roles of representatives at the national level and at the European level, the number of seats per country, and so on. The Act was to be followed by the adoption of uniform procedures for elections, including polling practices.

Unfortunately, these details have not yet been committed to paper, and the election rules of the member states have yet to be fully harmonized. In particular, there are differences in the counting of votes, the design of constituencies, the right to vote, eligibility for office, the terms and conditions of candidacy, the order of candidates on electoral lists, the allocation of vacant seats, election dates, and the verification of balloting results.

Laws regulating polls vary widely from country to country, and the Council of Europe has examined the question of whether efforts should be made to harmonize them. In 1984, Sir John Page of Britain and the nine members of the Parliamentary Assembly of the Council of Europe adopted the following motion (Worcester 1984, 6):

1. Considering that the activities of public opinion polls are now an established part of the election scene in West European states;

2. Believing that the growth of the polls is related to the growth of the electronic media and the declining importance of many traditional meetings and party activities;

3. Noting that opinion polls are widely and frequently reported by the media;

4. Considering that opinion polls provide more information for voters and enhance their awareness of the significance of their votes;

5. Noting the concern in some countries that polls may unduly influence the result of elections, particularly in the immediate pre-election day period;

6. Aware of the fact that in some countries there is a moratorium for the publication of opinion polls in the period of seven or three days before election day and that some national parliaments have already studied this problem;

7. Recommends that the Committee of Ministers invite the governments of member states to consider this matter with the objective of harmonisation.

On 2 July 1985, the Council of Europe unanimously adopted a report recommending that existing controls not be strengthened, but rather that self-regulation be adopted by requiring that polling organizations follow the rules established in existing codes of ethics, in particular that of the European Society for Opinion and Marketing Analysis and Research (ESOMAR) (Council of Europe 1985).

Thus, the Commission des relations avec les parlementaires nationaux et le public concluded that there were no grounds for attempting to harmonize member states' policies on polling. It did urge member governments, however, to promote adherence to codes of ethics so as to ensure a degree of fairness when the electorate is consulted, especially during the European elections (Antoine 1987).

The commission's conclusions are based, however, on rather unusual arguments concerning the influence of polls during elections. The commission stated that "as any information on the influence of polls on election results is subjective, there is no real proof of any interference in the democratic process" and that "the impartial publication of authentic opinion polls does not exert any noticeable or discernible influence on election results" (Antoine 1987, 81).

As shown in table 1.4, polling regulations in the 12 member countries of the Community vary significantly from one country to the next: Half the countries have no legislation banning the publication of pre-election polls, and the other half have established various forms of regulation. Portugal has the most restrictive legislation, followed by Greece, Luxembourg, Belgium, France and Spain.

**Table 1.4**
**Regulation of publication of polls in member states of the Council of Europe**

| Country | Period of prohibition |
|---|---|
| Germany<br>Denmark<br>Ireland<br>Italy<br>The Netherlands<br>Great Britain | No restrictions or minimal restrictions |
| Spain | 5 days before the vote |
| France | 1 week before the vote |
| Belgium | 2 weeks before the vote |
| Luxembourg | 4 weeks before the vote |
| Greece | No polls on television and, traditionally, no polls in the media 3–4 weeks before the vote |
| Portugal | No polls permitted for the entire election campaign |

*Source:* Updated and adapted from Antoine (1989, 32).

## Countries with a Minimal Degree of Regulation

### *Germany*

The case of Germany is interesting in several respects. First, even though Germany has no specific legislation prohibiting pre-election polls, its electoral law has regulated exit polls since 28 July 1979:

> 32(2) The results of opinion polls after votes have been cast may not be published before the expiry of the time prescribed for the election. [translation] (Germany 1986)

There is a fine of DM100 000, or approximately Cdn.$70 000, for offences under this section. It should be noted that section 5(1) of Germany's Basic Law states that:

> Everyone has the right to express and communicate opinions freely by means of the spoken and printed word or television broadcasts and to acquire information freely through generally available sources. Freedom of the press and freedom of information by radio and film are guaranteed. There shall be no censorship. [translation]

German legislators thus preferred to prohibit exit polls through the electoral law rather than to amend the Basic Law, which might have interfered with freedom of speech, or the law governing the press;

although the federal government is empowered to issue general rules on the status of the press (s. 75(2)), the law in question falls under the jurisdiction of the Länder. For these reasons, legislators rejected all proposals to ban polls in the days prior to the vote. For example, in November 1979, the vice-president of the Bundestag, Dr. Schmill-Volckenhausen, unsuccessfully proposed a ban on the publication and broadcasting of polls 10 days prior to election day. Thus, section 32(2) – the ban on exit polls – applies only to federal elections. (However, the state of Hesse adopted a similar provision for the local elections of July 1979.)

Lazareff (1984, 30) points out that although the federal assembly believed similar results could be obtained through self-regulation by polling organizations and the press, legislators tend to be somewhat distrustful of self-regulation: "The political class did not wish to take the risk of having the proper conduct of an election depend on the will of unscrupulous polling organizations or elements of the press."

A final interesting point concerns the polling organizations themselves. Since 3 July 1969, the major organizations have agreed not to conduct polls before federal elections to the Bundestag and not to publish or broadcast poll results in the 15 days prior to an election (Bogart 1985, 40).

### Great Britain

It was only in June 1968 that the publication or broadcasting of polls during elections came into question. Thus, in its recommendations to amend electoral law, the conference of the Speaker of the House of Commons proposed that "there be no broadcasting or publication by television, daily newspapers or magazines of opinion polls or projections of the election outcome for a period of 72 hours prior to the vote" (see *Sondages* 1977, 161). However, the British government rejected this proposal one month later: It was not convinced that the publication of opinion polls actually influenced election results.

The British Press Council criticized the proposal on two grounds. First, over the longer term, such rules would threaten freedom of the press: If some polls were disclosed during the last days of an election campaign, the press would be prevented from commenting on or discussing the information in question. Second, the Council foresaw a real danger that speculation and rumour would occur during election campaigns, which, in its opinion, could be much more dangerous than the publication of polls.

In 1982, Labour MP Dick Douglas introduced a bill in the House of Commons to ban the publication of all opinion polls during elections, regardless of subject. He also asked the secretary of state to oblige polling organizations and the media to disclose methodological information on every published poll: the sponsor's name, the number of interviewers, the cost of the poll, the complete wording of all questions, the number of respondents, the interview period, the sampling method and any other relevant information. The bill would also have established a commission to provide liaison between the Press Council, the British Broadcasting Corporation and the Independent Broadcasting Authority for purposes of monitoring the publication of opinion polls during elections. Any organization failing to comply with the rules would be subject to a fine of £400 (about Cdn.$1 000). The bill died on the order paper, however.

A second proposal, intended to amend the 1949 *Representation of the People Act* and limit the publication of polls during election campaigns, was advanced in July 1982 by members of the Select Committee on Home Affairs. The Committee as a whole, however, was more concerned with the issue of election expenses than the issue of polls. Finally, in March 1983, Labour MP Douglas Hoyle proposed that the publication or possession of all polls be banned for the election period (Worcester 1984, 4).

In 1986, the British Market Research Society set up an information telephone line with the aim of improving the public image of polls and helping journalists improve poll coverage. In 1987, the major British polling organizations (Gallup, Louis Harris, Marplan, MORI, and National Opinion Polls) reaffirmed their support for the International Code of Fair Practices in Market Research, adopted on 18 April 1971 by the International Chamber of Commerce. In addition, during the 1987 election, all British members of the Professional Association of Polling Institutes agreed to disclose their methodologies; they also prepared a guide on opinion polls for use by journalists.

### The "Moderate" Countries: France and Spain

France is a special case. On 19 July 1977, the National Assembly adopted legislation to control the publication of election polls during election periods only. An attempt five years earlier, on 19 December 1972, had failed after the Senate unanimously adopted a proposal by Étienne Dailly to ban the publication of polls during the last 20 days before election day; the proposal never reached the floor of the National Assembly (Boursin 1990, 250). The proposal did lay the groundwork for the so-called law of 19 July 1977, which was much broader in scope: It banned the publication of pre-election polls during the week prior to the election and established a polling commission to monitor the technical quality of polls published or broadcast and to interpret the Act's publication and broadcasting provisions.

France's case is unusual for another reason. Compared with the other democracies, the number of polls and surveys published and broadcast during pre-election periods, as reported by the polling commission, is astronomical: in 1988, there were 153 polls for the presidential election; 16 for the legislative elections; 2 for district elections; 8 for the referendum on New Caledonia; and 112 for municipal elections. Although the commission's work is limited to the pre-election period, there is a tremendous amount to be done. Accordingly, the commission has nine members, appointed for three-year terms by the council of ministers (section 6): three from the council of state, three from the court of appeal and three from the audit office. The staff consists of a secretary general, reporters and a consultant.

The order of 25 January 1978 states that the commission may appoint as reporters "public employees, magistrates from the judicial or administrative system, or individuals specially qualified in the field of opinion polls or the printed, spoken or television media" (s. 3). However, such individuals must have no administrative or financial ties with newspaper, polling or broadcasting companies (s. 4). Furthermore, no member of the commission shall have received any remuneration from a polling organization in the previous five years (s. 5).

The duties of the commission, as set out in section 5 of the Act, are extensive. In addition to ensuring the accuracy of polls, the commission has the power to define the provisions of polling contracts and to prohibit the publication of any poll concerning the second round of voting before the first round of voting has been completed. The commission is also responsible for maintaining open competition among the polling organizations and for preventing any "concerted actions, agreements, express or tacit understandings or coalitions in any form whatsoever, or for any reason whatsoever, hindering or restricting or liable to hinder or restrict the same activity by other persons or organizations" (France, *Loi du 19 juillet 1977*, 3837–38).[6]

An important feature of the Act is section 11, which bans the publication of polls during the week prior to an election. When an election requires two rounds of voting – such as the presidential election, where there is a period of two weeks between the first and the second ballot – organizations may publish polls during the second week of this period. The election period is much longer in France than in Canada's federal elections: the 1988 presidential election campaign, for example, lasted almost five months.

Under section 7 of the Act, all polling organizations must register with the polling commission, providing information on their corporate name and address and the name of the officer in charge. Any organization that does not register, but publishes a poll, commits an unlawful act.

Section 2 of the Act states that the publication or broadcasting of a poll must be accompanied by at least four items of information: the name of the organization that conducted the poll; the name and occupation of the sponsor; the number of persons polled; and the length of the interview period.

In addition, any member of the public who disputes the validity of a poll may file a complaint with the commission. During the 1988 presidential election, the commission received 17 complaints. Most of the complaints came from political parties, which had appointed representatives to monitor published polls and protect the interests of their candidates and their party (Gazier 1989). The commission also has broad investigative powers.

Polling organizations are also required by law to file a notice with the commission and to provide it with any additional information it may request. Thus, once an organization notifies the commission that it has conducted a poll for a sponsor and intends to make the poll public, the commission follows a series of relatively straightforward steps:

- Before a poll is published or broadcast, the organization responsible files a technical notice with the commission containing the information specified in section 3 of the Act: the purpose of the poll; the sample composition; the method of selecting respondents; the conditions under which interviews took place; the complete wording of the questions; the proportion of interviewees that did not respond to each question; the restrictions applying to interpretation of the results published; and the method used to arrive at any indirect results to be published. The commission may require that the organization accompany the publication or broadcast of any poll with one or more of these items, as well as those specified in section 2 of the Act.
- A reporter is assigned to the file (there may be as many as 12 reporters during election periods) and proceeds to monitor the information publicized in the media, to review the data supplied by the organization in question, and to set down observations about the poll and its subsequent use.
- Next, the file is submitted to the consultant, who also provides comments and observations and highlights the more contentious items. Since early 1981, the consultant has been Jacques Antoine, president of the Société de statistique de Paris and the Société de statistique de France.

- Once these two reports have been filed, the organization is often called upon to provide additional information. After a second examination, a report is submitted to the members of the commission. In cases where departures from the law or technical problems are noted, a meeting is held with the polling organization to clarify matters and to give the organization a chance to defend its work.
- A final report is prepared by the reporter, in some cases in conjunction with the consultant; the report is submitted to commission members, who decide what sanctions to impose. During the 1988 presidential elections, the commission issued 15 statements and instituted criminal proceedings in four cases. Between the date of its establishment and 10 March 1989, the commission issued some 105 statements (Crouzet 1985; Gazier and de Leusse 1988).

In practice, the application of the law does not appear to present major difficulties, and in the opinion of the chair, François Gazier, it has generally been respected; many cases have involved negligence rather than voluntary acts of fraud. However, the main difficulty does not arise from polling organizations that adhere strictly to the Act – and in this sense, the commission acts much more as adviser than monitor – but in their relations with the media, for they are the window through which people learn of the poll results. The commission's efforts in the past few years have therefore been directed more toward media management. In this regard, the commission is especially vigilant the first time a poll is published, then more tolerant when the information is repeated, for which it allows a reference or footnote (Gazier and de Leusse 1988, 14).

It is obviously difficult to say whether the quality of public opinion polls published and broadcast during French election campaigns has improved since the law came into force on 19 July 1978. According to the chair of the polling commission, the quality of the polls has improved over the years, the commission's expertise has been generally appreciated by polling organizations, and certain questionable activities have been eliminated because of the sanctions outlined in the Act. Some problems persist, especially in the adjustment of results (Gazier and de Leusse 1988, 13). It is more in the media and journalistic treatment of the polls that several weaknesses seem to persist, and there is still a great reluctance to publish or broadcast decisions or clarifications issued by the commission.

Everyone respects the ban on the publication of polls after the first round in the presidential election. Countries bordering on France also respect this regulation; what interest could they have in meddling in the internal affairs of their neighbours? In addition, the rate of penetration of foreign media is relatively low in France. This has given rise to a new phenomenon: the political rumour. Certain candidates and parties purportedly spent their time in 1988 spreading information that a particular candidate was ahead or behind, in an apparent attempt to bring out the vote. However, this phenomenon is not widespread.

In Spain, holding polls is a fairly recent phenomenon dating from the mid-1970s; publication of poll results is prohibited for a five-day period prior to voting day.

### Countries with the Most Restrictions: Belgium, Portugal and Greece

Following the example of France, on 18 July 1985 Belgium passed a law banning polls during the 30-day period prior to national and European elections. The text of the Belgian Act on the publication of opinion polls reads as follows:

> 5   From the thirtieth civil day preceding the date of one of the elections governed by the electoral codes or one of the elections to the European Parliament, it is prohibited to divulge, broadcast or comment on, by any method whatsoever, the results of polls related to these elections.

Furthermore, Belgian law is much more stringent than French law in the way it treats the methodology that must accompany the publication of a poll. Section 2 stipulates that 12 technical items must accompany published poll data:

> 2. The publication of an opinion poll shall be accompanied by the following:
>    a) a statement of the goal and purpose of the opinion poll, as well as the target population;
>    b) the number of persons participating as pollsters;
>    c) the size of the initial sample and number of persons actually interviewed;
>    d) the sampling method;
>    e) the composition of the sample of persons actually interviewed by sex, age, income and socio-professional standing, before and after a possible weighting, to the extent that these data were recorded during the poll;
>    f) a percentage breakdown of responses to all questions, with the percentage of persons who did not respond to each question, as well as the bases on which the various percentages were calculated;

g) general information on the interval of confidence used, given the size of the sample;

h) the manner in which the questions were asked: personal interviews in a public place, personal interviews at the home of the interviewee, telephone interviews, written surveys, etc.;

i) a classification of the sample by community size, with an indication of the number of communities in which persons were interviewed;

j) the name(s) and position(s) of the pollster(s);

k) a list of the questions asked, including the possible answers found in the questionnaire or verbally communicated to interviewees; and

l) the name of the organization or person sponsoring the poll.

On publication of the poll, this information must be deposited with the Institut national de la statistique.

The Act of 1985 also created an opinion poll commission with a mandate to propose, within the 12 months following promulgation of the Act, recommendations concerning "the standards of quality and rules of conduct to be observed by persons and organizations while conducting opinion polls, as well as methods of monitoring and respecting these standards and rules" (s. 3). This commission is composed of 13 members: nine specialists, at least two statistics professors and one civil servant from the Institut national de la statistique. Anyone violating the Act may be subject to a fine that could vary from 50 to 2 000 Belgian francs (approximately Cdn.$10 to $500). However, three years after the 1985 Act was adopted, the royal decree that was to establish these standards had still not been published and the Act was not always being respected, to the dismay of its initiator, Gaston Pâque, a socialist senator from Liège (Solinge 1988).

Section 60 of Portugal's election Act for the assembly of the republic bans "any broadcast of polls or surveys of voter attitudes toward candidates, from the date an election is called to the day after election results are known" [translation]. The Act specifies that elections are to be called by the president of the republic and that the length of the campaign is 21 days. According to Alexandre Lazareff (1984, 25), "The press has openly flouted this prohibition, publishing polls in the form of 'opinions' or analyses of the electorate and reprinting the results of polls published by Spanish newspapers. There has, however, been no official response to this conduct."

In Greece, the first polls were apparently conducted in 1946 by an Allied mission sent to supervise the referendum of 1 September 1946, held to enable Greek citizens to decide which political system to adopt (Jessen et al. 1947). But it was not until 1974, during the first free elections, that polls were used during a campaign. The Greek tradition is interesting: Although self-regulation is not discussed, the press in fact refrains from publishing poll results. In 1979, however, Prime Minister Georges Rallis came out in favour of tighter polling regulations during elections. Greek law prohibits the broadcasting of poll results on television.

### OTHER COUNTRIES: AUSTRALIA, JAPAN, REPUBLIC OF KOREA, SRI LANKA, BRAZIL AND SOUTH AFRICA

Over the past few years, several other countries have enacted legislation to regulate polling during elections. Australia, for example, has provisions in its election Act banning the publication of polls for 48 hours prior to a federal election (Ley 1976, 51). Australia is unique in two respects. For 30 years (1941–71), Gallup was the only polling firm in the country; its polls were published by the media associated with the Herald group, based in Melbourne. In 1971, the person in charge of Gallup's polls for this group founded his own polling organization, the Roy Morgan Research Centre. In 1973, the Herald group engaged the firm of McNair Anderson and Associates to conduct polls for them using the method developed by George Gallup. Since then Australia has been the only country with two Gallup polling firms: Morgan Gallup Poll (1941) and Australian Public Opinion Polls (The Gallup Method) (1973) (Beed 1977).

Other countries, including the Republic of Korea, Sri Lanka and Japan, also have legislation banning the publication of poll results (Herman and Mendel 1977, 82). Japan's various laws and regulations pertaining to the organization of the two legislative bodies and regional elections were codified in 1950 into a single document, which stated that elections had to be held in a fair and honest manner. In 1981, the law was amended in an effort to reduce costs occasioned by changes in the political situation in Japan. Electoral law now applies to the conduct of elections, advertising and the activities of interest groups. In 1983, the Act was amended again to regulate the duration of election periods. More recently, a delegation visited France to learn about the French experience (Gazier and de Leusse 1988).

Japan's election Act has the following section on polls:

138(3) With respect to elections, no person shall publicize the results of popularity polls or opinion poll results or trends predicting who will gain an official government position. (For senatorial candidates running in proportional elections, in particular, this section applies to the number and identity of persons belonging to political organizations or parties.) [translation]

More recently, the publication and broadcasting of polls has been prohibited in Brazil since the reintroduction of democratic elections. In South Africa, polls are banned for the last 40 days of an election campaign.

## NEW POLLING TECHNIQUES: EXIT POLLS

Over the years, and despite the best efforts of legislators, new polling techniques have appeared that are not always covered by legislation. Several countries have already witnessed the emergence of various procedures and methods, some of which have been put into practice: the tele-questionnaire, minitel surveys and focus group techniques used at various times in a campaign. A symposium held in Toronto from 9 to 11 November 1990 by the American magazine *Campaigns & Elections* demonstrated that human imagination is limitless. Therefore, we think it important to examine these new practices or technologies because they will affect the conduct of elections, if they have not already done so.

The exit poll is a new technique, introduced over the past few years, that has quickly become both widespread (especially in the United States) and controversial. The name has in fact changed over the years, with CBS calling them "election-day polls" and NBC using "street polls," then "election-day polls" and finally "exit polls" (Mitofsky 1991, 99). Exit polls are mainly a television phenomenon; the top priority of the networks has been to jockey for first place in the race to report election results. For several years now, the media have concentrated mainly on analysing electoral districts and polling stations that they consider good indicators of the eventual outcome to enable their political journalists to project results based on comparisons with votes cast during previous elections.

Thus, exit polls have become the latest tools for predicting election results before the polls close, especially in the United States (Sudman 1986, 331). Efforts to predict voting results are not new; what is different is the idea of interviewing people right after they have cast their vote, while the election is still going on.

During the 1960 presidential election in the United States, Senator Barry Goldwater, a Republican from Arizona, introduced a bill to prohibit radio broadcasts of election results before midnight the night of the election. Media predictions of Goldwater's defeat in the 1964 presidential election and Richard Nixon's 1972 victory gave rise to several bills aimed at banning premature broadcasting of election results

(Calmes 1984, 565). Some countries, including the Federal Republic of Germany in 1979, have enacted legislation to ban this practice, considering it a violation of the principle of the secret ballot.

The issue underlying the debate about exit polls is whether voters, having seen the results of exit polls on television, will behave differently than they would otherwise have done (Mendelsohn 1966, 213). This question is obviously related to the hypothesis of the rational voter, which posits that people will vote or be interested in an election to the extent that they believe the benefits of voting outweigh the costs. Although such benefits – as perceived by voters – may take various forms, they are related to the following factors:

- the voter's perception of the relative importance of an election;
- the voter's perception of the proximity of election day; and, more generally,
- the voter's sense of civic duty or the relative importance attached to the right to vote in a democratic system.

The costs associated with this process may also be extremely varied:

- conflict with other activities with greater priority (e.g., work, recreation);
- time required to vote (e.g., the distance to be covered to reach the polling station); and
- discomfort and inconvenience (e.g., waiting in line before voting).

As election day approaches, however, interest in voting normally increases, which in turn should promote greater voter turnout (Wald 1985, 275). Similarly, broadcasting election predictions or results before the polls close may discourage people from voting, even if they had intended to do so; the attempts of party workers to encourage their fellow citizens to go to the polls may thus be fruitless. The broadcasting of exit polls may also:

- swing the vote toward the winning party or candidate (the bandwagon effect);
- swing the vote toward the losing party or candidate (the underdog effect);
- persuade some individuals to vote, although they had not intended to do so originally.

To understand the U.S. debate about exit polls, we must recognize that the question goes beyond polling to the central issue of broadcasting of results on election day. The same holds true for Canada. In his study of the 1964 presidential election, Harold Mendelsohn conducted panel surveys before and after the polls closed: on 2 November, immediately before the election and after the polls closed; and on 3 November, the morning after the election. Mendelsohn interviewed 2 270 people from a sample of 3 400 registered voters in California (rate of response: 66.8 percent) in the first round of interviews and a further 1 724 voters in the second round. Mendelsohn studied voters' responses on three main variables:

- voter commitment to specific candidates before election day;
- the extent of their exposure to election information through the electronic media the day before election day; and
- their voting intentions.

In the first set of interviews, 1 704 respondents stated that they intended to vote; in the second round, 1 689 said that they had indeed voted. Of the 1 212 voters in the original sample who had been committed to specific candidates, 97 percent said they had voted for the candidate of their choice. Only 14 respondents, representing less than 1.2 percent of the sample, said they had changed their choice. Among the 1 689 individuals who voted, 475 (28.1 percent) said they had voted after 4:30 PM Pacific time, which means that they could have been exposed to media predictions about the results; only 196 (41.3 percent), however, reported seeing or hearing such predictions.

The study showed that among respondents who had intended to vote for Johnson or Goldwater, 97 and 96 percent, respectively, did in fact support the candidate of their choice. With respect to the undecided voters, 50 percent voted for Johnson, 28 percent voted for Goldwater, and 22 percent remained undecided (Mendelsohn 1966, 218). Mendelsohn concluded that being exposed to certain predictions did not change respondents' voting intentions, nor did it cause a massive swing to the candidate predicted to be the future president. He concluded that televised broadcasts from the eastern United States did not result in any bandwagon or underdog effect among California voters. The effect on undecided voters, however, is difficult to determine with any accuracy.

Mendelsohn's conclusions were corroborated by a study by Douglas A. Fuchs, who examined the effects on voting of actual disclosure of election results on radio and television. Fuchs (1966, 235) showed that exposure to the media and to projections had absolutely no effect on either turnout or public opinion about a given candidate: 95.5 percent of respondents who had seen media projections before the election actually cast votes, as opposed to 96 percent of those who saw them only after voting. Among those who changed their vote, a slightly higher proportion had seen media coverage before voting (3.5 percent, compared with 1.8 percent).

It was the 1980 presidential election, however, that prompted the most heated controversy. In an unprecedented turn of events, California voters learned almost three hours before the polls closed that Ronald Reagan had been elected president of the United States. It was 5:15 PM Pacific time, two hours and 45 minutes before the polls closed, when Jimmy Carter telephoned Ronald Reagan to concede the election to him (Perry 1984, 162). California voter turnout was down by more than 2 percent relative to the previous election (Calmes 1984, 565). A debate ensued about the legitimacy of using exit polls to predict election results. The fact that by 10:00 PM Eastern time the networks can accurately predict the outcome of an election may make voting an exercise in futility for people in the western United States. There is no consensus, however, about the actual impact of such projections.

The problem can be approached in several different ways. Most studies emphasize that the 1980 presidential election was unique. Philip L. Dubois, for example, examined changes in California voter turnout during presidential elections between 1960 and 1980. Turnout fell constantly over these two decades, from 83.7 percent in 1960 to 70.8 percent in 1980 (Dubois 1983, 355). In addition, the two most significant drops in turnout took place in 1972 (down by 4 percent) and 1980 (down by 4.5 percent), years when the results of exit polls were disclosed. However, in 1964 and 1968, years when no projections were broadcast, turnout fell by only 1.3 percent and 2.2 percent, respectively.

Other authors, among them Joseph Nocera, contest the scientific value of exit polls. Nocera points out, for example, that ABC was to select only one voter in three for its sample; however, in its haste to meet quotas (and presumably to beat other networks to the punch), the network interviewed almost all voters coming out of selected polling stations, even going so far as to question individuals employed there. Nocera also emphasized the difficulties of interviewing certain types of voters and the fact that young voters tend to agree more readily to answer questions, which skews the results (Nocera 1984, 42).

The main difficulty, however, lies not in methodology but in the fact that the media misuse election results when they declare the winners before the polls are closed. This is the opinion of Burns W. Roper, president of the Roper Organization, who says that exit polls should not be used because the public feels they interfere with the normal course of an election. In addition, he believes that this practice has little effect on the reputation of the polling institution and that any benefits that may be gained by predicting the winner half an hour before the other television networks are not worth the risks incurred in doing so. Richard Salant, vice-president of NBC, says that his network would never broadcast projections based on exit polls because the results may be distorted or subject to manipulation (Milavsky et al. 1985, 14).

Opponents of exit polls will find a certain amount of support in a study by Jackson (1983) that suggests such polls may have a slight effect, not so much on voters supporting a losing candidate, but on those supporting a winning candidate (Sudman 1986, 338). In his review of the literature, Seymour Sudman (1986) concluded voter turnout drops by between 1 and 5 percent in electoral districts where the polls close after 8:00 PM Eastern time.

Delli Carpini (1984) found that the broadcasting of projections had a relatively weak effect on presidential and congressional elections. He also found that voters with higher incomes, more education and white-collar jobs seemed to be most highly influenced. Although the overall effect seems too small for us to conclude that projections affect the outcome of presidential elections, congressional elections in 14 districts were won by smaller majorities than estimated by exit polls conducted in these districts.

On the other hand, those in favour of exit polls, like CBS vice-president Ralph E. Goldberg, say that if journalists and the media start making decisions about the merits of certain information, such as that contained in exit polls, a dangerous precedent would be established that could jeopardize the credibility of the television networks. Banning the broadcasting of projections might also be unconstitutional.

Where the debate will lead is not clear. If exit polls are conducted properly and the methodology is not in question, the central question that remains is whether the broadcasting of results influences voter turnout. Studies show that exit polls do have some effect on voter turnout; with respect to election results, however, or at the very least voting intentions, the effect is much less. Sudman (1986) concluded that the question of whether this effect is significant remains much more a political than a statistical debate.

All of this discussion of exit polls is interesting because of its implications for Canada: British Columbia is in a situation similar to that of California. Nobody is contesting the validity of exit polls as a means of confirming election results and as post-election studies. Recent failures in the United States during the November 1990 elections diminished the popularity of surveys of this type as a tool to predict election results. A survey conducted among 10 000 voters for the three major television networks and the Cable News Network met with insurmountable technical problems, to the point where the results obtained were useless (Porado 1990).

## CONCLUSION

A comparison of the various laws and provisions covering polling during elections indicates that the list of countries that have imposed a partial or total ban on polls during elections is much longer than might be expected and is getting longer. Regulations provide for blackouts varying from 48 hours to the entire duration of the election period. France, Belgium and New York State also require that the methodology and results of published or broadcast polls be filed with a commission or board of elections. Although exit polls are highly controversial, only Germany has banned the broadcast of their results.

Publication or broadcast of specifications sheets for polls or the various methods used is also a concern of various lawmakers. Belgium is, to our knowledge, the country that has gone farthest in this direction. It requires publication of 12 methodological elements. The laws governing elections in New York State indicate that eight such elements must be published. French law mentions only four such elements: the polling institution responsible, the sponsor, the number of persons interviewed and the interview period. In New York State, all polls are included in election expenses; the candidate, party or organization that has sponsored the poll must also report the cost of polling.

A review of the legislation of various countries reveals that governments tend toward outright banning of polls near the end of election campaigns rather than requiring the publication of a specifications sheet. Only France has chosen both options. However, every law is imperfect and can only partially regulate as multifaceted a practice as polling.

# 5

# *SELF-REGULATION, CODES OF CONDUCT AND ETHICS*

Sᴇʟꜰ-ʀᴇɢᴜʟᴀᴛɪᴏɴ is often cited as the best way to improve the quality of both written and broadcast reports of public opinion polls. Germany provides a good example of self-regulation: polling organizations and broadcast associations there have decided not to make the results of any polls public during the 15 days immediately preceding election day. Other countries, such as France, have opted for a mixed approach: the state imposes certain restrictions but leaves the task of defining standards for the presentation of polls to the organizations involved.

In this chapter we assess proposals for self-regulation offered by researchers, pollsters, journalists and broadcasters. We analyse the various codes of ethics proposed by or in effect in these professions, particularly since neither the public nor the pollsters themselves are familiar with many of them. We have two objectives: to clarify how various organizations think polls should be published; and to outline the main limitations to the observance of these standards. This enables us to propose a typical analysis grid containing the main items of information that should accompany the publication and broadcasting of any poll and to examine the ethical aspects of polling (Stoetzel 1980; Sadouin 1973). But first, we shall present and describe the main codes that we have listed.

## UNIVERSITY RESEARCHERS

University researchers have long been concerned with the ethics of research. This is seldom a public concern, because the discussion tends to be philosophical and theoretical, delving into the very foundations of research. If researchers in the natural sciences were the first to explore these concerns, researchers in the social sciences are now equally preoccupied with the ethics of research, particularly since the development of investigative techniques using the scientific method.

In 1976, the Canada Council published a report by an advisory committee on survey research for use by researchers and public or private funding organizations in the field of social sciences (Canada, Consultative Group 1976). The study dealt primarily with university research and presented recommendations to improve the quality of polling while protecting the rights of the participants and reducing the risks of solicitation of certain groups. The report's conclusions are discussed in the section of this chapter entitled "Freedom and Information: The Right to Privacy."

On another front, associations of university researchers, such as the Regroupement québécois des sciences sociales (RQSS), whose members include the Société québécoise de science politique and the Association canadienne des sociologues et anthropologues de langue française, have been trying for more than a decade to impress upon journalists and the media generally the importance of presenting polling methodology along with polling results to assist the public in evaluating the validity of the data and accompanying commentary.

In 1979, the polling committee of the RQSS published a document entitled *Sondages politiques et politique des sondages au Québec*, containing several recommendations about the publication of polling results during election periods. In particular, the RQSS recommended that certain information about the methodology used should accompany the publication or broadcasting of all poll results. In addition, the committee stated that polls are one of many sources of information that influence public opinion during election campaigns. They help promote public debate by allowing electors to situate their own opinions on various subjects vis-à-vis those of the majority. But for polling organizations and journalists alike, the greatest challenge is to ensure that the questions asked and the information made public are both pertinent and valid. For this reason they must be verifiable and comparable. The committee therefore suggested that all poll results be accompanied by a survey specifications sheet outlining the significant methodological elements of the poll:

1. The identity of the client. (For whom was the poll conducted?)
2. The identity of the polling organization. (Who conducted the poll?)
3. The period of the poll. (Between what dates were the interviews conducted?)
4. The description of the population. (What was the target population?)
5. The sampling method. (How were the sample individuals selected?)

6. The response rate. (What is the ratio between the number of participants in the survey and the total sample after those deemed ineligible are excluded?)
7. The number of questionnaires completed.
8. The data-collection method. (Was it by telephone or personal interview?)
9. The wording of the questions.
10. The number of respondents per 100 percent block. (What is the number of participants on which the percentages for each column and each category were calculated?)
11. The number and method of distribution of non-respondents. (Will they hypothetically behave the same way as undecided voters?)
12. The projection method. (If the number of seats is predicted, how was this derived?)
13. The accuracy of the headlines. (Do they correspond to what the polls say?)
14. The signatures of those responsible for the poll.
15. The margin of error.

The committee also recommended that all data and reports of polls published or broadcast be legally deposited so that everyone has access to them (Lachapelle et al. 1989, B-3).

Since the Quebec referendum of May 1980, members of the associations represented on the polling committee have questioned whether these recommendations should be extended to election periods. The discussion continues in the Quebec university community: the most hotly debated issue is whether polls should be banned in the week preceding election day. Some believe that the law should ban not only public opinion polls, but also the broadcasting and publishing of all electoral advertising. Others, like political scientist Vincent Lemieux of Université Laval, oppose any form of ban on the grounds that it would contravene democratic principles and the free exchange of information (V. Lemieux 1988, chap. 5).

Over the last few years, but particularly since the 1988 federal election, the polling committee of the RQSS has concentrated on seeing three of its recommendations implemented:

1. that the broadcasting or publication of all polls be accompanied by methodological information to allow the public to judge their quality and reliability;
2. that all data, reports and information linked to polls published

or broadcast during election periods be accessible to the public; and

3. that a polling commission be established with the primary function of verifying the validity and reliability of polls broadcast or published during election periods.

## POLLSTERS AND POLLING ORGANIZATIONS

The question of ethics in polling is not new. As early as 1944, George Gallup, a pioneer of opinion polling, emphasized that all methodological information should be made public at the time a poll is published or broadcast to enable the public to judge the poll's quality (Gallup 1944, 1972).

Similarly, in 1948, the Standards Committee of the American Association for Public Opinion Research (AAPOR) proposed a first code of ethics for the profession. The code was in two sections: a code of professional practices, and a description of the proper content of research reports. Research reports should contain seven elements:

- the objective of the poll;
- the names of those by whom and for whom the poll was conducted;
- a general description of the target population, and the size and description of the sample;
- the weighting or adjustment methods;
- the dates when the interviews were conducted;
- the method of collection;
- an adequate description of the personnel and control methods used.

Reports should also include the questionnaire and the results, the database on which percentages were calculated, and the distribution of the interviews (AAPOR 1948–49).

Although the World Association for Public Opinion Research (WAPOR) adopted the code at its September 1948 congress, it was not until June 1960 that the Council of AAPOR adopted it. In 1977, AAPOR added to its code some broadcasting standards for reporting of poll results, recommending, for example, that members of the media demand such information from those commissioning and conducting polls.

There is also an International Code of Fair Practices in Market Research, which was prepared jointly by the International Chamber of Commerce (ICC) and the European Society for Opinion and Marketing Analysis and Research (ESOMAR) and adopted on 18 April 1971 (Lazareff

1984). WAPOR also subscribes to it. Amended in 1976, the code establishes rules of conduct by which the polling organizations must abide when dealing with interviewees to maintain both the confidence of the public and that of their clients. In addition, the code requires that any report issued by a polling organization contain details on a list of technical points similar to those suggested by AAPOR. In some countries, such as France, adherence to these rules is assured not only by ESOMAR's member organizations but also by the Chambre syndicale des sociétés d'études et de conseils (Syntec), whose members include the major polling organizations. In 1981, this group published a code of practices on survey research entitled *Code de pratiques loyales concernant les panels et les enquêtes répétitives.*

In Canada, the Canadian Advertising Research Foundation (CARF) and the Canadian Association of Marketing Research Organizations (CAMRO) established similar standards. CARF offers its marketing studies and research clients a consultation and evaluation service to ensure that survey methodology and questions conform to professional standards (Canadian Advertising Research Foundation 1984). CAMRO, whose membership includes the principal polling organizations in Canada, audits its members to verify the quality and reliability of the methods they use or develop and to ensure that they abide by the established standards of the profession. For example, the Quebec affiliate of CAMRO, the Association de l'industrie de la recherche marketing et sociale (AIRMS), proposed that specifications sheets for a survey be published *separately* when polling results are published and that the methodology sheet include 13 essential elements (Association de l'industrie 1991, 8–9):

- The name of the research firm responsible for the survey. If the fieldwork was executed by a sub-contractor or by another entity, the name of such should also be published.
- The name of the project manager as well as his or her status in the firm.
- The name of the client for which the survey was conducted, as well as the department within this company that has ordered the survey.
- The description of the population under study including all the relevant specifications (i.e., adults, Canadian citizenship, language, regions or territories, etc.).
- The sampling method and the type of sampling (original sample frame, selection process of households and individuals, number of callbacks, with or without substitution, with or without stratification, type of stratification).

- The rate of response calculated as per AIRMS standards.
- A verification of the representativeness of the weighted sample (sex, age, region, language and other relevant variables).
- The weighting procedure, where applicable (i.e., regional adjustment, weighting on the size of household, etc.).
- The survey method. If by telephone, the number and location of the telephone centrals, the proportion of work validated and the type of validation will be disclosed. If interviewing was computer-assisted it will be mentioned and the proportions of calls monitored indicated.
- The interviewing period.
- The duration of a typical interview and list of the main sections of the questionnaire as well as their logical sequence.
- The maximum margin of error based on a 95% confidence level.
- The relevant warnings indicated in the report by the researcher (i.e., a vote intention is not a forecast, etc.).

## JOURNALISTS

On 21 August 1967, the British Press Council rejected a recommendation by a British parliamentary committee on electoral reform that suggested prohibiting the publication or broadcasting of opinion polls during the 72 hours preceding an election. According to the Council, imposing such a rule would constitute a blow to the freedom of the press, because it was not the publication of polls and accompanying commentary that was the target of the rule, but the form and the manner in which polls were presented and broadcast. The Council also considered it a dangerous precedent to allow the state to dictate how certain types of information could be presented, a precedent that would open the door to other forms of censorship (British Press Council 1977, 163–64).

For this reason, the British press adopted a code of conduct in 1970 to forestall action by the government along these lines. The code requires that published poll results be accompanied by information about the size of the sample, the date of the poll, the methodology, and the number of non-respondents. These rules apply only to reported poll results, not to any commentary on the poll that might be published.

By 1979, the British Royal Statistical Society was examining whether the press was abiding by these rules. Its observation was that, in general, the British press was respecting the standards, with the exception of polls from the Gallup organization, which frequently omitted the rate of non-response. The society noted, however, that problems occur when articles are paraphrased, that is, when poll results are republished in another paper. In these situations, the code of conduct also falls by the wayside.

In Canada, the Canadian Daily Newspaper Publishers Association (1980) considered the responsibility of journalists in analysing and reporting opinion polls and proposed a list of questions journalists should ask themselves whenever they receive poll results, be it a private or a public poll. This checklist for journalists contains 12 questions closely related to the criteria published by the American Association for Public Opinion Research. The objective of the questions is to enable journalists to identify the various methodological aspects of a poll; each of these elements should accompany the publication of a poll:

1. Who commissioned the poll?
2. Who was interviewed?
3. How were the interviewees selected?
4. How many people were interviewed?
5. What was the response rate?
6. How accurate are the results?
7. Who conducted the interviews?
8. How were the interviews conducted?
9. When did the interviews take place?
10. What were the exact questions asked?
11. Are the presentation titles and texts exact?
12. Are the results pertaining to only one section of the sample clearly indicated?
   (Canadian Daily Newspaper Publishers Association 1980)

Prime Minister Joe Clark proposed in February 1980 that polls be banned during an election period. The Quebec press council responded by reiterating the position it had taken on pre-election polling on 17 May 1979. The press council reaffirmed its belief that the public's right to information is better served by greater rigour and integrity on the part of the pollsters and journalists than by any form of legislative action. The council also stated that legislative intervention could be the prelude to other forms of state censorship and lead eventually to restrictions on the circulation of free and complete information (Conseil de presse du Québec 1980).

The council emphasized, however, that poll results should be accompanied by verified and verifiable information to ensure that they cannot be used for partisan purposes by individuals or groups. Such information would include all pertinent methodological information, such as the sample size and composition, research and survey methods, and data-collection methods. With this technical information in hand, members of the council and the public would be in a better position to evaluate the quality of a poll. Thus, although the council rejected state regulation, it recognized that judging the quality of a poll requires information about how it was produced.

In its presentation to the Royal Commission on Electoral Reform and Party Financing, the Quebec Federation of Professional Journalists (QFPJ) urged recognition of the principle that information should always be current, accurate, presented fairly and drawn from diverse sources and that this principle should apply during electoral periods as well. While recognizing that opinion polls published in newspapers are not always accompanied by all the information necessary to allow readers to assess their quality, QFPJ believes that the role played by organizations such as the polling committee of the Regroupement québécois des sciences sociales and AIRMS remains the best method of regulating polls. The federation also stated that section 98.1 of Bill C-79 represents a dangerous precedent that could eventually endanger freedom of the press. According to QFPJ, the content of an article or newspaper report should not be determined by the state. Self-regulation is, therefore, the preferred route; at the same time, pollsters, academics and even political adversaries should have an opportunity to express an opinion on the validity of any poll.

In a recent work on journalism, Pierre Sormany notes the need for caution in interpreting polls that are not accompanied by a survey specifications sheet and those based on samples of relatively homogeneous groups (for example, the Conseil du patronat, the Fédération des caisses populaires). In such cases, reporters must always make sure the sample is representative and examine the context in which the poll was conducted. For these reasons, Sormany argues, any article or report of a scientific nature should be accompanied by certain information: the name of the sponsor, the size and composition of the groups studied, the method of selection, the questionnaire or a description of the survey, the details of the results obtained, the experimental mortality, the means and other scientific values used, and the possible explanations of the correlations obtained (Sormany 1990, chap. 11).

## BROADCASTERS

Canadian broadcasters have also developed rules for broadcasting poll results. By the mid-1970s, the Canadian Broadcasting Corporation (CBC) was already considering how much time it should devote to pre-election polls and how to differentiate between polls with no scientific value and other polls (Canadian Broadcasting Corporation 1975, 83–98). The network therefore developed rules for broadcasting polling results and began to require that the results of any reported poll be accompanied by the following information: the name of the sponsor, the polling organization, the dates of the interviews, the data-collection method used, the target population of the survey, the type of sample and its size, the margin of error, the limits of the poll, and the wording of the questions and the order in which they were asked. In addition, the titles of polling reports were to be neutral.

The CBC guidelines emphasized the need to exercise careful judgement about the validity of polling results and their journalistic use during election periods; at the same time, however, they recognized that the characteristics of radio and television programming would likely require different approaches to the treatment of polls. On television, for example, technical advances in the presentation of graphic images have made it easier to present polling results and other statistical information in a dynamic, lively way without losing the viewer's interest. On radio the opportunities are more limited, particularly in the case of newscasts, where time is a major constraint. Thus, the news editor becomes a crucial participant in the process; the editor must be able not only to synthesize the results but also, like any other journalist, to judge the validity of the poll and to translate the results into readily digestible news copy.

In its presentation to the Royal Commission, CBC also outlined its policy on opinion polls. The CBC policy requires that when poll results are aired, greater prominence be given to the data than to interpretations of the data and that the name of the polling organization, the client, the sample size, the date of the poll, and the margin of error all be included in the report on the results (Canadian Broadcasting Corporation 1990):

### SURVEY RESEARCH AND POLLS

Surveys and polls are techniques for gathering data. They are applied to the discovery of facts, the uncovering of attitudes, and the verification of hypotheses. The data collected by surveys and polls constitute the basis of various studies and reports published by governments, pressure groups, researchers or journalistic organizations. To ensure the validity and reliability of their results, survey research and polls must be conducted according to tested and recognized standards. Any departure from such standards or other relevant information on the techniques or funding of such research should be made known to the public.

### A. CBC-Conducted Polls and Surveys

The CBC assumes full responsibility for the operation and quality control of the surveys it decides to conduct.

All survey or polling initiatives must be authorized in advance by the Director of Information Programs who must also approve personally or through his/her authorized delegate the final questionnaire.

The CBC Research Department must participate in all the steps of the survey, from original design to the interpretation of the results, and must assume the responsibility of ensuring the highest standards.

The CBC will not commission or conduct polls to be broadcast during the last 10 days of an election or referendum campaign. This does not preclude the commissioning of polls during such a period when they are strictly for post-election broadcast.

B. **Broadcasting Results of Other Surveys and Polls**

1) Prior to broadcasting results of any non-CBC survey or poll, the CBC journalists concerned are expected to:
   a) obtain all necessary data on the methods used, as well as the main results of the survey or poll;
   b) obtain a range of interpretation if differences exist;
   c) in the case of public opinion polls, obtain the opinion of the research department as to the validity of the methods used and the interpretation of the results.

2) In broadcasting results of polls and surveys, the actual data must be given prominence over interpretations of that data.

   Report the name of the person or organization conducting the poll, and where relevant the political party affiliation if any, the name of the sponsor if any, the size of the sample, the period during which the survey was conducted and the margin of error.

3) Special care must be exercised in the presentation, whether live or pre-recorded, of statements gathered through interviews with randomly selected persons in a given situation (such as convention delegates), or phoned in by general invitation to the audience of an open-line program. Comments so gathered must be presented for the sole purpose of illustrating the range and texture of popular opinion. Care must be taken not to suggest that such presentations reflect the distribution or weight of opinion in the community on one or another side of a question. Similarly, while the contents of the comments may be summarized, under no circumstances must any numerical tally of comments received on either side of a topic be given.

The CBC stated that although it does not sponsor or conduct polls whose results would be broadcast within 10 days of the end of an election or referendum campaign, it would not refrain from broadcasting the results of other polls during this same period. In this instance, however, reporters must have verified the validity and interpretation of the results and must supply the poll's survey specifications sheet. In the case of interviews or telephone surveys, reporters are urged to be vigilant and to make clear that the opinions expressed are only illustrative and should not be taken as representative.

The Association canadienne de la radio et de la télévision de langue française (ACRTF), to which some 125 private stations belong, also told the Royal Commission that broadcasters should be free to air poll results, regardless of whether they commissioned the poll. Although the ACRTF (1990) emphasized that certain rules must be followed in such broadcasts, it did not specify what those rules should be. The association decided in November 1990, however, to set up the Conseil canadien des normes de la radiodiffusion, which will receive and review listeners' complaints (Delisle 1990). The council, established in January 1991, has six members: three representatives from the industry and three from the general public.

In its statement to the Royal Commission, the Canadian Association of Broadcasters (CAB) argued that, in requiring that all polls be accompanied by methodological information, Bill C-79 would have favoured the written press (1990). The CAB did not explain exactly how broadcasters would be placed at a disadvantage, but it argued that any regulation in this field would constitute an attack on freedom of expression. The association was also concerned that efforts to regulate opinion polls might result in their disappearance from news bulletins and public affairs programs. The CAB would, therefore, prefer self-regulation within the profession. Its code of ethics, like that of the Radio and Television News Directors Association of Canada, recognizes the principle that broadcasters must do everything they can to ensure that all information, including polls, receives equitable treatment.

## GOVERNMENTS AND ELECTION CANDIDATES

The only participants in polling with no defined code of ethics for conducting, publishing, broadcasting and disclosing polls during an electoral period are governments, political parties, interest groups and electoral candidates. The former have the public funds to conduct electoral polls for their own purposes and to make the results public during election or referendum campaigns. And there is nothing to prevent a party leader, an advocacy group, a candidate or a party organizer from releasing the results of an internal poll without revealing the complete contents of the poll report.

Instances of partisan use of poll data by party leaders, candidates and organizers are common. For example, during the 1988 federal election campaign, in an article that appeared in the Montreal *Gazette* on 8 November 1988, Prime Minister Mulroney admitted that the polls placed his party last, but he stated that the 12-point spread in the most recent Gallup poll was erroneous: "The Conservative party's pollster, Decima Research Ltd., has found different standings. They indicate an entirely different conclusion – a tight race that is getting even tighter" (Kennedy 1988). Furthermore, Marcel Côté, an official of the Progressive Conservative party in Quebec, stated that such polls "influence the dynamic of the campaign and create problems for the party organizations" (Lavoie 1988). Nevertheless, the Prime Minister's press secretary, Marc Lortie, indicated that the Progressive Conservative party had no intention of making its own poll public. If the media were subject to strict rules, this issue would have been resolved somewhat differently. Perhaps the poll would not have been published with insufficient technical information.

Despite the existence of a polling commission, France also experiences shortcomings of this type. During the last presidential campaign, the television station Europe 1 broadcast a poll attributed to Renseignements généraux, giving Jacques Chirac the victory on the second ballot. In addition, in the course of an interview on the program "L'Heure de vérité," Charles Pasqua, minister of the interior, stated that the confidential polls by Renseignements généraux favoured the candidate of the Rassemblement du Peuple pour la République. Many, including the director of political studies for the Société française d'enquête par sondage, Jérôme Jaffré, whose own institute's polling results differed from those reported, saw this kind of reporting as a major challenge to the polling commission. In the final analysis, the commission has few means of controlling attempts at misinformation and political manipulation of public opinion.

Nevertheless, in a document published subsequent to these events, the polling commission reaffirmed that it had "the strongest reservations concerning rumours about polls that are presented as confidential" and that the law prohibits "the publication or the broadcasting of a poll over which the commission can exercise no control." When Renseignements généraux refused to abide by the commission's rules of conduct, Syntec-Études de marché, the professional organization of France's opinion polling institutes, made an unsuccessful attempt to have the 1977 law amended.

It would, therefore, appear essential that all legislation and regulations governing public statements about polling results during electoral periods apply not only to polling organizations but also to governments. Invoking confidentiality to justify revealing only partial results of a poll, particularly during an election campaign, is unacceptable. New York State's *Fair Campaign Code* stipulates that any poll mentioned during an election campaign must be made public to preserve honesty and fairness in the campaign. Governments, and the men and women in politics, would do well to reflect on the meaning of the old Anglo-Saxon concept of fair play; and governments in Canada should equip themselves with precise rules to control the publication and broadcasting of survey and poll results, both during and outside electoral periods.

### FREEDOM AND INFORMATION: THE RIGHT TO PRIVACY

In the past few years many countries have devoted greater attention to protecting citizens from unauthorized use of computerized files, and especially from the abuses that can arise when data files are cross-accessed for purposes other than the administrative uses for which the information was originally gathered.

The Canada Council's advisory group on polling surveys, which reported in 1976, raised the question of the individual's right to privacy. Every citizen has the right to refuse to respond to a survey. When a person agrees to respond, however, the confidentiality of the information gathered must be maintained, and it is up to the researcher, as well as the person or organization storing the data, to eliminate all risk that the data's confidentiality will be jeopardized. Moreover, most universities in Canada have an ethics committee to ensure that all research projects meet established ethical standards. The advisory group formulated the following requirements:

1. the respondents are aware of and approve the objectives of the project, as well as the use to which their answers will be put;
2. the survey ensures the anonymity of the respondents and protects the confidential nature of the answers; and
3. there was prior agreement in principle with the respondents about the use and re-use of the data. (Canada, Consultative Group 1976, 1.28)

Thus, the advisory committee recommended that respondents be informed clearly of the objectives and sponsor of a survey or poll and assured of the confidential nature of the data gathered. Moreover, the committee proposed that the following form accompany all interviews:

Our purpose in asking you these questions is (to be filled in for each case). The answers with any identifying information connected with them will be seen only by (the number and status of the few, if any, individuals who must know for the success of the project). Your name will then be removed from the information you give, so that for all other purposes this information is anonymous. The whole set of anonymous answers, as given by you and many other informants, is to be deposited in (name of survey centre) for scientific use by other researchers; this may save you the bother of answering the same questions over again at some later date. (Canada, Consultative Group 1976, 1.39)

The report also deals with data used by the researcher and their accessibility to other groups, be they researchers, respondents, organizations or individuals. Furthermore, the advisory group suggests that the results of all polls should become public property and that the organization funding the research should assume part of the cost of storing the results in a data bank. University data banks should be considered "as custodians of resources whose value extends far beyond the bounds of the universities where they are kept" (Canada, Consultative Group 1976, 1.22). Any researcher requesting a grant should be advised of these terms and conditions. To our knowledge, this recommendation has not been made policy, probably for financial reasons.

In France, the collection and subsequent treatment of nominal data are regulated by the Commission nationale informatique et liberté (CNIL) (Law 78-17 of 6 January 1978). In any survey, census or poll, interviewees must be informed of their right to refuse to participate in the survey or to refuse to answer questions, and must be advised of the consequences of their refusal. Interviewees must also be told who will see the information they provide, that they have the right to see their basic personal data at any time, and that they also have a right to correct the information. Computerized files of nominal data that could permit identification of an individual's background; political, philosophical or religious opinions; or union status cannot be kept longer than two months.

According to Jacques Antoine (1985, 94), however, the CNIL's role is the source of numerous conflicts because its rules apply to everything except polls. This has caused many conflicts between pollsters and legislators. This is the case, for example, with respect to the pollster's obligation to obtain prior written consent from each participant. This is no doubt feasible in the case of personal or mail surveys, which are often used in France and in Europe generally; but for telephone interviews this is completely impractical, although it would be possible to establish procedures to obtain participants' verbal consent initially and later their written permission to use the information collected for scientific purposes. The requirement that all nominal information be destroyed also makes it practically impossible to conduct panel surveys over a period exceeding two months.

## CONCLUSION

Theoretically, establishing ethical standards and codes of conduct is sufficient to ensure the self-regulation of university researchers, pollsters and polling organizations, journalists, broadcasters, governments and candidates for election in the matter of publishing and broadcasting election polls.

Most of these professions have a code or set of standards in place:

- **University researchers**
- The advisory report on surveys and polls for researchers and public or private organizations funding research in the social sciences (Canada, Consultative Group 1976);
- *Sondages politiques et politique des sondages au Québec* (Comité des sondages of the Regroupement québécois des sciences sociales 1979).

- **Pollsters and polling organizations**
- Code of ethics (American Association for Public Opinion Research 1960, amended in 1977);
- Code of ethics (World Association for Public Opinion Research 1978);
- The International Code of Fair Practices in Marketing Research (International Chamber of Commerce, Association européenne pour les études d'opinion et de marketing 1971, modified in 1976);
- Code of Practice for Opinion Polls (British Market Research Society 1970);
- Code of ethics (Canadian Advertising Research Foundation 1984);
- Code of ethics (Canadian Association of Marketing Research Organizations (AIRMS 1991)).

- **Journalists and broadcasters**
- Code of conduct (British Press Council 1970);
- Journalist's checklist (Canadian Daily Newspaper Publishers Association 1980);
- Rules for the publication or broadcasting of poll results (Canadian Broadcasting Corporation 1975);

- Code of ethics (Canadian Association of Broadcasters);
- Code of ethics (Radio and Television News Directors).

Finally, we note that, in January 1991, the Canadian Association of Broadcasters and the Association canadienne de la radio et de la télévision de langue française established the Canadian Broadcast Standards Council to address ethical standards.

Paradoxically, then, only governments and candidates for election remain without an established code of ethics on the use of polls. Despite reservations about regulating the publication and broadcasting of polls, journalists and broadcasters seem to agree that:

- certain technical information must accompany polling results, particularly the name of the person or organization that conducted the poll, the name of the sponsor, the size of the sample, when interviews were conducted and the margin of error; and
- except for those of the CBC, there are no rules prohibiting the publication or broadcasting of a poll in the days immediately preceding an election.

Codes of ethics or conduct have the same limitations as legislation: they cannot cover all the aspects of polling. For example, during the 1988 federal election campaign, it was revealed that a polling organization had purportedly conducted a survey for an Ontario television station and then used these same data for the Liberal Party of Canada. It is reprehensible for a polling organization to use the results of a survey commissioned by one of its other clients, with or without that client's consent, for partisan purposes. Various codes address the main problems that have been observed. However, a gap remains when it comes to protecting persons interviewed for polls and, more specifically, protecting the confidentiality of the data gathered. Although many codes of ethics exist, political educators, pollsters and the media must continue the discussion on the standards to follow during election campaigns; such a dialogue would probably settle many difficulties. Unfortunately, this thinking is at the embryonic stage, despite efforts made over the past several years.

# 6

## ANALYSIS OF SURVEY REPORTS FROM POLLING ORGANIZATIONS DURING THE 1988 FEDERAL ELECTION CAMPAIGN

~

POLLING FIRMS WERE among the first to establish codes of ethics. As we saw in the last chapter, for example, in 1948 the standards committee of the American Association for Public Opinion Research proposed a code of ethics that explicitly described the items that must be included in a survey report. In this chapter we analyse the content of polling organizations' survey reports to determine whether various organizations adhere to the standards they have set for themselves. Our objective is not to point a finger at a particular polling firm but rather to note the strengths and weaknesses of these reports and to offer pollsters some points for reflection. These documents are seldom available to the general public, who rarely ask for them. Yet, they often contain information communicated to clients, who are often the media, and they form the basis for journalistic reporting and analysis. For this reason alone, the survey reports warrant examination.

To begin our analysis of survey reports we compiled an inventory of all Canada-wide polls conducted during the 1988 federal election campaign. Each polling organization was then asked to provide detailed reports on the surveys they had conducted. Using the analysis grid proposed by the Regroupement québécois des sciences sociales (presented in Chapter 5), we studied the content of these reports. We chose this grid rather than those proposed by AIRMS, newspaper publishers or broadcasters because it amalgamates all of the criteria contained in the other codes. Moreover, this formulation is the most recent (1988); consequently its criteria better reflect the evolution of the practice of polling. It is no more constraining or limited than other codes, with the exception of the one proposed by the broadcasters, which has fewer criteria.

## ACCESSIBILITY OF SURVEY REPORTS

In all, 22 Canada-wide polls were made public in the course of the 1988 election campaign, a significant increase over 1984 when there were only 12.[7] To these must be added 37 regional and constituency polls, for a total of 59 polls published during the campaign. This total, however, remains well below the 73 polls conducted during the British election of 1987 (Butler and Kavanagh 1988, 125). During election periods, many Canadian newspapers and broadcasters commission or sponsor polls by various polling organizations. As a general rule, political parties and governments commission opinion surveys from these same firms; these polls are rarely made public. Newspapers and broadcasters in

**Table 1.5**
**Cross-Canada polls conducted during the 1988 federal election campaign**

| Dates of survey | Polling organization | Sponsor | Report available |
|---|---|---|---|
| 1–2 October | Gallup Inc. | *Toronto Star* | Yes |
| 2–3 October | Angus Reid | Southam News | Yes |
| 2–10 October | Environics | *Globe and Mail* | Yes |
| 6–13 October | Insight Canada Research | CTV | No |
| 7–12 October | Canadian Facts | CBC/Radio-Canada | Yes |
| 12–15 October | Gallup Inc. | Subscribers | Yes |
| 13–20 October | Insight Canada Research | CTV | No |
| 20–22 October | Gallup Inc. | *Toronto Star* | Yes |
| 25–26 October | Environics | *Globe and Mail* | Yes |
| 26–27 October | Angus Reid | Southam News | Yes |
| 26–29 October | Gallup Inc. | Subscribers | Yes |
| 27–30 October | Insight Canada Research | CTV | No |
| 28–30 October | Environics | *Globe and Mail* | Yes |
| 2–5 November | Gallup Inc. | Subscribers | Yes |
| 3–8 November | Environics | *Globe and Mail* | Yes |
| 3–8 November | Angus Reid | Southam News | Yes |
| 3–10 November | Insight Canada Research | CTV | No |
| 5–8 November | Canadian Facts | CBC / "The National" | Yes |
| 9–12 November | Gallup Inc. | *Toronto Star* | Yes |
| 14–17 November | Gallup Inc. | *Toronto Star* | Yes |
| 15–17 November | Angus Reid | Southam News | Yes |
| No dates | Insight Canada Research | CTV | No |

Canada seldom have their own polling facilities; they too use the services of the polling organizations. The exception is perhaps the CBC, which has its own research department.

It took only a single telephone call from an official of the polling committee of the Regroupement québécois des sciences sociales to obtain 17 of the 22 survey reports produced during the 1988 election campaign. Only the five reports produced by Insight Canada Research could not be obtained, despite numerous requests (see table 1.5).

We should also note that the research department of the Canadian Broadcasting Corporation and its collaborator, the Canadian Facts Institute, are in a somewhat different category. Not only did we receive the reports on the two polls conducted by CBC/Radio-Canada, we also obtained the questionnaires and the computerized data. Given that the CBC is a public corporation, it must, to a certain extent, be answerable to the public. But there seems to be an internal rule, particularly in the English service of the CBC, that forbids the disclosure of any polling data within 30 days of broadcast. This practice is particularly troubling if it applies during an election period. How else can the public evaluate the validity of a poll?

## CONTENT ANALYSIS OF SURVEY REPORTS

The first notable observation about the information presented in table 1.6 is the significant variation in voting intentions revealed by the surveys. When the aggregate of all poll results is examined, it becomes clear that intentions to vote for the Progressive Conservative party were underestimated by about 4.5 percent, whereas intentions to vote for the Liberals or NDP were overestimated by 0.3 and 5.5 percent, respectively.

If we consider only the last three polls conducted during the final week of the campaign, we see that the picture is a little different, although the trend remains identical: the Progressive Conservative vote was underestimated by 2 percent, and the Liberal and NDP votes were overestimated by 0.9 and 2 percent, respectively, within the margin of error. In the case of the other parties, it is difficult to trace voting intentions from the accounts in the written press. In six polls this information was not available; the fact that they were broadcast polls does not justify this oversight. On the whole, however, the vote for the other parties was underestimated by 0.7 percent earlier on and by 1.5 percent in the final days of the campaign.

The paradox of the 1988 campaign was that the results of the first and the last polls of the campaign came closest to the actual vote recorded on 21 November. The first Gallup poll of the campaign forecast the

**Table 1.6**
**Canada-wide voting intentions**
(percentages)

| | Progressive Conservative | Liberal | NDP | Other | Undecided/ refused | N |
|---|---|---|---|---|---|---|
| 1. Gallup Inc. 1–2 October | 43 | 33 | 22 | 3 | — (16) | 1 061 |
| 2. Angus Reid 2–3 October | 45 (34) | 26 (20) | 27 (20) | 2 (2) | — (24) | 1 512 |
| 3. Environics 2–10 October | 42 (38) | 25 (22) | 29 (26) | 5 (4) | — (10) | 1 515 |
| 4. Insight Canada Research 6–13 October | 46 | 27 | 26 | — | — (18) | 1 100 |
| 5. Canadian Facts 7–12 October | 42 (36) | 25 (22) | 29 (25) | 4 (3) | — (14) | 2 467 |
| 6. Gallup Inc. 12–15 October | 39 | 29 | 28 | 4 | — (18) | 1 027 |
| 7. Insight Canada Research 13–20 October | 43 | 25 | 30 | — | — | 1 100 |
| 8. Gallup Inc. 20–22 October | 40 | 28 | 29 | 3 | — (19) | 1 034 |
| 9. Environics 25–26 October | 33 (27) | 31 (26) | 28 (23) | 8 (7) | — (17) | 811 |
| 10. Angus Reid 26–27 October | 35 (27) | 35 (27) | 28 (22) | 2 (1) | — (23) | 1 502 |
| 11. Gallup Inc. 26–29 October | 38 | 32 | 27 | 3 | — (11) | 1 034 |
| 12. Insight Canada Research 27–30 October | 35 | 39 | 23 | — | — | 1 100 |
| 13. Environics 28–30 October | 31 (27) | 37 (32) | 26 (23) | 6 (6) | — (13) | 727 |
| 14. Gallup Inc. 2–5 November | 31 | 43 | 22 | 4 | — (10) | 1 041 |
| 15. Environics 3–8 November | 35 (32) | 37 (33) | 24 (21) | 5 (4) | — (9) | 1 275 |
| 16. Angus Reid 3–8 November | 39 (31) | 35 (27) | 24 (18) | 2 (2) | — (22) | 1 501 |
| 17. Insight Canada Research 3–10 November | 39 | 39 | 21 | — | — (15) | 1 120 |
| 18. Canadian Facts 5–8 November | 38 | 38 | 21 | — | — (8) | 2 200 |

Table 1.6 (cont'd)
**Canada-wide voting intentions**
(percentages)

| | Progressive Conservative | Liberal | NDP | Other | Undecided/ refused | N |
|---|---|---|---|---|---|---|
| 19. Gallup Inc. 9–12 November | 35 | 35 | 26 | 4 | — (8) | 1 026 |
| 20. Gallup Inc. 14–17 November | 40 | 35 | 22 | 3 | — (12) | 4 067 |
| 21. Angus Reid 15–17 November | 41 (37) | 33 (30) | 23 (21) | 3 (2) | — (11) | 1 512 |
| 22. Insight Canada Research Dates not available | 43 | 32 | 20 | — | — (15) | 2 720 |
| Mean: all polls | 38.8 | 32.7 | 25.2 | 3.8 | | |
| Mean: last 3 polls | 41.3 | 33.3 | 21.7 | 3.0 | | |
| Election results: 21 November 1988 | 43.3 | 32.4 | 19.7 | 4.5 | | |

Note: N = number of respondents. The numbers in parentheses reflect respondents' intention-to-vote before redistribution of "undecided" respondents. The total of the results for each party, as published in the media, does not always add to 100%; polling organizations should follow the established method of rounding off numbers.

election results more accurately than the last Gallup and Angus Reid polls conducted during the final week of the campaign. In other words, if the ups and downs of the campaign, including the leaders debate, are discounted, the question that remains is whether there really was an election contest at all. The lowest score for the Progressive Conservatives was registered subsequent to the leaders debates, which took place on 25 October in French and 26 October in English; according to Environics and Gallup polls soon after that time, the Conservatives had the support of only 31 percent of the electorate. The Liberals' best performance was 43 percent in the Gallup poll conducted between 2 and 5 November, which gave them a 12-point edge over the Conservatives. The wide spread in this poll provoked controversy about its reliability, because no other organization had found 40 percent support for the Liberals at any point during the campaign.

The significant fluctuations in the number of undecided voters recorded by the various polling organizations also raised questions.[8] On average, Angus Reid found the greatest number of undecided voters (20 percent). It is difficult to understand, however, how this number could have declined to only 11 percent in Reid's last poll, when it had hovered at 24, 23 and 22 percent in the three preceding polls. For Insight Canada Research, in three of its five polls that provided this information, the average proportion of undecided voters was 16 percent, varying between 15 and 18 percent. The Gallup average was 12 percent: the highest was 19 percent prior to the leaders debate, and the lowest was 8 percent. The Environics average was also 12 percent, with a range of 9 to 17 percent. Finally, Canadian Facts recorded an average of 11 percent undecided: its two polls indicated 14 and 8 percent. These variations in the percentage of undecided voters indicate that methodology differed from one polling organization to another.

A more detailed analysis of the 17 available polling reports (see table 1.7) reveals several observations about the extent to which organizations supplied information considered essential to a complete description of methodology, results and analysis.

### General Information

*Identity of the Sponsor*
The Canadian Institute of Public Opinion (Gallup) is the only organization that never discloses the name of its sponsor or sponsors in polling reports. This practice is not unique to Canada; as we have seen previously, the British Institute of Public Opinion has been criticized for the same reason. It is, nevertheless, surprising that only Gallup does not reveal this information, or at least its subscription list. Sponsors are clearly identified in the other polling reports: Angus Reid is commissioned by the Southam News chain; Environics by the *Globe and Mail*; and Canadian Facts by CBC/Radio-Canada. This criterion was met in the majority of cases observed.

*Identity of the Polling Organization and Signature on the Reports*
Lorne Bozinoff and Peter MacIntosh always sign Gallup's polling reports. In the case of Angus Reid, reports are not signed, although they appear under the name Angus Reid. Environics presents a unique situation. Those responsible for the polls in 1988 actually signed the articles that appeared in the *Globe and Mail*; Michael Adams, Donna Dasko and James Matsui all signed articles appearing at various times in the daily, a practice that was discontinued after the 1988 election. Environics was also identified.

### Description of Methodology

*The Questionnaire and Wording of Questions*
Canadian Facts was the only polling firm to send us complete questionnaires for their polls. Unfortunately, complete questionnaires were

**Table 1.7**
**Analysis of polling organizations' reports**

| | Sponsor | Collection method | Initial sample | Ineligible people | Rejection rate | Respondents | Response rate | Margin of error | Sampling method | Wording of questions |
|---|---|---|---|---|---|---|---|---|---|---|
| 1. Gallup Inc. 1–2 October (N=1 061) | No | Yes | No | No | No | Yes | No | Yes | No | French English |
| 2. Angus Reid 2–3 October (N=1 512) | Yes | Yes | No | No | No | Yes | No | Yes | Yes | English |
| 3. Environics 2–10 October (N=1 515) | Yes | Yes | No | No | No | Yes | No | Yes | Yes | English |
| 4. Insight Canada Research 6–13 October (N=1 100) | Report not available | | | | | | | | | |
| 5. Canadian Facts 7–12 October (N=2 467) | Yes | Yes | No | No | No | Yes | No | Yes | No | French English |

Table 1.7 (cont'd)
Analysis of polling organizations' reports

| | Sponsor | Collection method | Initial sample | Ineligible people | Rejection rate | Respondents | Response rate | Margin of error | Sampling method | Wording of questions |
|---|---|---|---|---|---|---|---|---|---|---|
| 6. Gallup Inc. 12–15 October (N = 1 027) | No | Yes | No | No | No | Yes | No | Yes | No | French English |
| 7. Insight Canada Research 13–20 October (N = 1 100) | Report not available | | | | | | | | | |
| 8. Gallup Inc. 20–22 October (N = 1 034) | No | Yes | No | No | No | Yes | No | Yes | No | French English |
| 9. Environics 25–26 October (N = 811) | Yes | Yes | No | No | No | Yes | No | Yes | Yes | English |
| 10. Angus Reid 26–27 October (N = 1 502) | Yes | Yes | No | No | No | Yes | No | Yes | Yes | English |
| 11. Gallup Inc. 26–29 October (N = 1 034) | No | Yes | No | No | No | Yes | No | Yes | No | French English |

**Table 1.7** (cont'd)
**Analysis of polling organizations' reports**

| | Sponsor | Collection method | Initial sample | Ineligible people | Rejection rate | Respondents | Response rate | Margin of error | Sampling method | Wording of questions |
|---|---|---|---|---|---|---|---|---|---|---|
| 12. Insight Canada Research 27–30 October (N = 1 100) | Report not available | | | | | | | | | |
| 13. Environics 28–30 October (N = 727) | Yes | Yes | No | No | No | Yes | No | Yes | Yes | English |
| 14. Gallup Inc. 2–5 November (N = 1 041) | No | Yes | No | No | No | Yes | No | Yes | No | French English |
| 15. Environics 3–8 November (N = 1 275) | Yes | Yes | Yes | No | No | Yes | No | Yes | Yes | English |
| 16. Angus Reid 3–8 November (N = 1 501) | Yes | Yes | No | No | No | Yes | No | Yes | Yes | English |
| 17. Insight Canada Research 3–10 November (N = 1 120) | Report not available | | | | | | | | | |

**Table 1.7** (cont'd)
**Analysis of polling organizations' reports**

| | Sponsor | Collection method | Initial sample | Ineligible people | Rejection rate | Respondents | Response rate | Margin of error | Sampling method | Wording of questions |
|---|---|---|---|---|---|---|---|---|---|---|
| 18. Canadian Facts 5–8 November (N= 2 200) | Yes | Yes | No | No | No | Yes | No | Yes | No | French English |
| 19. Gallup Inc. 9–12 November (N= 1 026) | No | Yes | No | No | No | Yes | No | Yes | No | French English |
| 20. Gallup Inc. 14–17 November (N= 4 067) | No | Yes | No | No | No | Yes | No | Yes | No | French English |
| 21. Angus Reid 15–17 November (N= 1 512) | Yes | Yes | No | No | No | Yes | No | Yes | No | English |
| 22. Insight Canada Research not available (N= 2 720) | Report not available | | | | | | | | | |

*Note:* "Yes" indicates that information was provided in a polling organization's report, "no," that it was not.

not part of the survey reports we received from Gallup, Angus Reid and Environics. According to Claire Hoy (1989), Angus Reid differs from the other polling organizations in that it asks which of the three leaders is the most popular before asking which of the parties the respondent supports. In addition, Reid asks the question on voting intentions at the end of the questionnaire, whereas Environics, for example, asks it at the beginning.

It would seem that the principal reasons for variations in reported voting intentions have to do with the way polling firms ask about voting intentions and subsequently redistribute the "other" responses in a poll. In the first case, as shown in table 1.8, most of the polling firms use two questions to elicit the respondent's voting intentions. First, respondents are asked which party they intend to support. If the answer is "undecided," a follow-up question asks which party they would most likely support. Only Angus Reid proceeds differently; that poll asks only one question, which explains why Reid's rate of undecided voters is higher than that of the other organizations. It does not, however, explain variations in the polls conducted at different times during the campaign. With respect to allocating "other" responses, no polling organization makes a distinction between respondents who intend to refrain from voting, intend to spoil their ballot, do not know how they are going to vote, or refuse to answer (Lachapelle 1986). The first two instances are hardly cases of indecision, given that the respondents have expressed a clear opinion; nor should these respondents be asked the follow-up question.

Two examples illustrate this difficulty. In the report on the first Canadian Facts/CBC poll, it is evident that respondents who had no intention of voting were included in the "undecided" category (Canadian Broadcasting Corporation 1988, 19). In addition, the voting intentions presented in table 1.6 exclude those who stated they would not vote or would spoil their ballot; in fact, before the follow-up question, the "undecided" rate was at the same level as that of the Angus Reid poll, at 24 percent. An analysis of the first Environics poll conducted during the campaign shows that the figure for abstentions and spoiled ballots was comparable to support for smaller parties, at 4 percent; but this category disappeared after the follow-up question, as it did in the case of the Canadian Facts/CBC poll. In both of these cases it would be interesting to know whether the follow-up question was asked. Gallup and Angus Reid lump all the "other" responses in one category

Thus, the genuinely "undecided" electors are those who insist they do not know what party they are going to vote for or who refuse to answer. The polling organizations' treatment of "undecided"

**Table 1.8**
**Questions on voting intentions**

| Polling organization | Question |
| --- | --- |
| Gallup Inc. | Si l'élection fédérale avait lieu aujourd'hui, quel serait le parti du candidat de votre choix? |
| | Si indécis ou refus, demandez: |
| | Même si vous n'avez pas encore fait votre choix, quel parti êtes-vous le plus porté à appuyer dans le moment? |
| Angus Reid | Thinking of how you feel right now, which party's candidate will you be most likely to support in the upcoming federal election? |
| Environics | If a Canadian election were held today, would you vote for the candidate of the ...? |
| | Undecided on the previous question ... |
| | Would you say that at the present time you are at least leaning or slightly favourable to one of the parties? |
| Canadian Facts | Si des élections fédérales avaient lieu aujourd'hui, pour quel parti voteriez-vous? |
| | Aux personnes qui n'ont pas identifié de parti à cette question... |
| | Actuellement, quel parti seriez-vous tenté d'appuyer? |
| Insight Canada Research | Reports not available |

respondents varies considerably and may actually misrepresent reality, particularly when all voting intentions add up to 100 percent of respondents, yet abstentions and spoiled ballots have disappeared as categories. Is this a true picture of the actual number of "undecided" voters, or are the poll and accompanying commentary presenting a distorted picture of public opinion?

Moreover, and somewhat surprisingly, given that these were Canada-wide polls, only Gallup's reports present the survey questions in both official languages. Some rather clumsy wording is apparent in both versions of the Gallup question on voting intentions (see table 1.8). In the case of Canadian Facts/CBC, we received a report from the Montreal office with the wording of the questions in French and one from Toronto with the questions in English. There is a different emphasis, however, in the French and English versions: in the former, the emphasis is on "quel parti" ("which party"), while in the latter it is on the "party's candidate."

### Data-Collection Methods

All the organizations clearly indicated their data-collection methods; all use only the telephone, except Gallup. In a departure from usual practice during the 1988 election campaign, Gallup conducted its surveys both by telephone and in face-to-face interviews. Of the seven Gallup polls during the campaign, two were conducted by telephone, four in face-to-face interviews, and one using both methods. In our view, combining two methods poses numerous problems, especially when the results are presented together without comparing telephone results with those obtained through personal interviews.

### Sampling Methods

Only Gallup did not supply complete information about the selection of respondents. The Environics report on its first poll of the campaign described its method as follows: "Environics uses a multi-stage stratified sampling procedure. The number of interviews in each province is in proportion to the population of the province. Similarly, communities are broken down into five groups by size – from rural to urban – and the number of interviews for each group reflects its proportion of the population" (Adams et al. 1988a). Canadian Facts/CBC states that it uses a probability sample, randomly generated by computer; the Angus Reid report refers to a random sample.

Each sampling method (random, quotas, stratified, iterative) has its limits. Because telephone polls are the common practice in Canada, most of the organizations use random and stratified sampling and a selection grid to choose the persons they wish to interview in each household.

To select respondents randomly, most of the organizations use randomly generated telephone numbers (a practice that can increase the number of rejects), the telephone directories of major Canadian cities, or in certain types of polls, the voters list, even though it does not list every individual eligible to vote. In some countries, like Belgium, where voting is mandatory, electoral lists do permit random sampling of the electorate because every citizen of voting age is automatically listed (Javeau and Vigneron 1989, 73–77).

In the case of quota and stratified samples, researchers are given a form indicating the number and the characteristics of the people they must question (Whalen 1970, 148–49; Boursin 1990, 241–44). One might be asked, for example, to contact 10 to 12 people, equal numbers of women and men: four between the ages of 18 and 29, four between 30 and 49, and two 60 or over. In designing these samples, care must be taken not to apply too many variables, which would render it

difficult, if not impossible, to find people with all the requisite characteristics. One must also take into account, particularly in door-to-
door surveys, the fact that certain people are likely to be more accessible
than others at different times of the day. There is always some "invol-
untary bias" in these samples because it is up to the interviewer to
choose the respondents.

Random and stratified methods are essentially North American
practices. In Europe, partly because their political tradition encourages
it, people much prefer to talk to the interviewer in person. Most polls
are therefore conducted face to face, using the quota method. Every
method has its drawbacks, however; no practice is inherently superior
to any other. The art of polling is, therefore, a question of knowing the
biases associated with each method and exercising appropriate controls.

## Response Rate

Whatever the collection method used, one must know the characteristics of the population selected and the size of the initial sample in order
to judge the relative success of a poll. Several factors may lead to the
exclusion by the pollster of some of those selected to be in the initial
sample: for example, disconnected telephones; a call answered at a non-
residential address; a call answered by a person unable to speak either
English or French; a call to a person whose disability prevents them
from answering; or a call answered by someone who is not eligible to
vote. These cases constitute the "rejections," which will be excluded
from the final sample. In the 17 reports we reviewed, this information
was missing.

The final sample is, therefore, composed of all the residential phone
numbers or addresses where eligible voters were found.[9] This is why
"selected population" and "sample population" are defined differently
in the polling reports: Gallup speaks of "adults 18 years and over,"
Angus Reid of "Canadian voters," and Environics of a "sample of
eligible voters." Voting eligibility depends on three factors: a voter must
be 18 years or over, a Canadian citizen, and not a member of any group
that does not have the right to vote. Only one poll, that conducted by
Environics between 3 and 8 November, specifies that the initial sample
was composed of 1 745 respondents; the other 16 reports did not mention
the size of the final sample at all (which is not the same as the actual
number of persons interviewed).

Once the basic information is known, some members of a household may be excluded from the final sample because they refuse to
participate (refusal by household or individual); or the selected individual is absent or ill, backs out during the interview, or is simply

impossible to reach after several attempts. When this occurs, it is important to know what efforts the researcher made to complete the survey.
How many calls or visits were made to contact non-responders or to
persuade those who refused to answer on the first try? These efforts
have an effect on the response rate; from a theoretical perspective, four
calls at different times of day are necessary to preserve the integrity of
the sample. This information was not given in any of the 17 reports
examined.

The rejection rate, which is the percentage of ineligible persons in
the initial sample, and the response rate, which is the number of people
in the final sample who completed the questionnaire, were also missing
from the reports. Yet this information is easy to compile; if the sample
is made up of 1 678 people and 200 are ineligible, then the rejection rate
is 11.9 percent, and there would be 1 478 people in the final sample. If
1 000 people from this group responded to the survey, the response
rate would be 67.7 percent. Even the CBC did not supply the number of
questionnaires completed.

### Margin of Error

All polling organizations specified that their margin of error falls within
a precise range. To evaluate the margin of error or the degree of confidence, we need to know whether this calculation was based on the
entire final sample or on the number of respondents. Polling organizations generally base the calculation on the number of respondents.
The formula is relatively simple. If we assume, very conservatively,
a dichotomic distribution of the population into two equal groups
($P_0 = .50$) for a confidence threshold of 95 percent ($P'$), we can use the
following formula, in which $N$ is the number of respondents:

$$\text{Margin of error (\%)} = P' \pm 1.96 \sqrt{\frac{P_0(1 - P_0)}{N}} \times 100$$

Thus, for 1 000 individuals, the calculation would be made like this:

$$\text{Margin of error} = \pm 1.96 \sqrt{\frac{.5(1 - .5)}{1\ 000}} \times 100 = \pm 3.5\%$$

Some statistical tables have even more precise margins of error,
depending on the distribution of responses.

In general, polling organizations in Canada use this formula or a
variation of it to calculate their margins of error. However, they do tend
to use standard margins of error calculated for samples of 800, 1 000,
1 200, 1 500 or 2 000 respondents. The margins of error stated in their

reports and subsequently published in the press are therefore not precise calculations, but approximations. For example, in all the Gallup polls except the last one of the campaign, the margin of error was stated as 4 percent, whereas the number of respondents was 1 061, 1 027, 1 034, 1 034, 1 041 and 1 026. Thus, if $N$ equals 1 000 and the interval of confidence is 95 percent, the margin of error should be ± 3.1 percent. In Gallup's last poll of the campaign, the reported margin of error was ± 3 percent when it should normally be ± 1.6 percent on a total sample of 4 067 respondents.

The margins of error published by the other polling organizations were calculated precisely. It should be understood, however, that this margin of error represents the "minimum" margin of error of a poll because not all interviewees respond to all questions; as a result, $N$ may be much less than the initial $N$, depending on the question asked. For example, in the case of voting intentions, the margin of error is much greater than the margin of error for the entire sample. As we will see, this problem becomes even more acute when the press publishes selected regional results.

### Adjustment and Weighting Methods

Results must be adjusted or weighted when the sample population is not comparable to the selected population. If we know, for example, that the population is composed of 52 percent women and 48 percent men, but the unadjusted sample contains 54 percent women and 46 percent men, the sample must be adjusted by assigning different weights to the women's and the men's responses. This is a common practice in Canada. In France, however, the various attempts to adjust samples have been subject to the scrutiny of the polling commission. For example, the vote of people surveyed during the previous presidential campaign is often used as an adjustment variable. We will not deal here with attempts to adjust for non-response to the voting intentions question, which in itself raises numerous questions (Tremblay 1986).

Unfortunately, none of the reports from the polling organizations satisfactorily described how they weighted their results. The Gallup report does not mention the subject. The Environics report states that their results are weighted to ensure "that they are in line with Statistics Canada data on the demographics of the Canadian population." Canadian Facts and Angus Reid adjust their results according to the sex and age composition of the population in each province. Canadian Facts also reports that other weighting factors were used in its first poll of the campaign: "In British Columbia, Ontario and Quebec additional weights were added for Vancouver, Toronto and Montreal to adjust their relative significance. The Montreal sample was also adjusted to represent francophones and anglophones according to the expected proportions. Finally, the weight of each province was allocated by its actual proportion" (Canadian Broadcasting Corporation 1988, 2). In Angus Reid's first poll, conducted on 2 and 3 October, the British Columbia sample, which was actually 173, was weighted to 228 so that each province would have a sample of about 400. Angus Reid did not use this procedure in its other polls.

A simple reading of the reports reveals that, despite the standards polling organizations have established, there are always several technical elements missing from the reports. Those elements would permit a satisfactory evaluation of the methodology and adjustment techniques used in conducting polls. The initial and final samples should be stated, a copy of the questionnaire should always be included, and a detailed description of the sampling plan should be presented.

## Presentation of the Results and Analysis

Polling reports vary greatly in length and in depth of analysis. Gallup, for instance, presents all its data in percentages only; we never find actual survey results. Their analysis is based solely on a description of these various percentages. Although Angus Reid offers more tables, the analysis remains essentially descriptive. In the case of Environics, the articles in the *Globe and Mail* report the central points of their analysis and contain a large number of computer-generated tables.

The use of cross-Canada polling results to predict regional voting intentions has become widespread in the last few years. Predictions of the number of seats each party would win, although less widespread, were also made during the campaign of 1988. In this study, we comment on these two types of analysis only.

### Predicting Regional Voting Intentions

The practice of presenting regional voting intentions has been around for several years and became widespread during the 1988 federal election; all the reports, except those of Gallup, offered regional data. The reports from Environics, Angus Reid and Canadian Facts included the size of the regional samples (N) on which estimates were based, as well as the results before adjustment for non-responses. The regional voting intentions in table 1.9 are those presented in the 15 reports that supplied this kind of data.

During the 1988 federal election campaign, members of the Manitoba wing of the Progressive Conservative party complained about the results of the Environics poll published in the *Globe and Mail* on 1 November (Adams et al. 1988b). A table presented "regional trends"

**Table 1.9**
**Regional voting intentions**
(percentages)

| Polling organization, date and number of respondents | Region | Progressive Conservative | Liberal | NDP | Other | Undecided/ refused |
|---|---|---|---|---|---|---|
| 1. Gallup Inc. | Atl. | 53 | 37 | 11 | 0 | |
| 1–2 October | Que. | 44 | 34 | 20 | 3 | |
| *(N = 1 061)* | Ont. | 34 | 39 | 25 | 1 | |
| | Prairies | 53 | 22 | 19 | 6 | |
| | BC | 39 | 25 | 29 | 7 | |
| 2. Angus Reid | Atl. (139) | 53 (40) | 34 (26) | 12  (9) | 1 (1) | — (24) |
| 2–3 October | Que. (405) | 56 (40) | 20 (14) | 23 (16) | 1 (—) | — (29) |
| *(N = 1 512)* | Ont. (533) | 36 (28) | 32 (25) | 30 (23) | 1 (1) | — (22) |
| | Prairies (268) | 50 (38) | 23 (18) | 22 (17) | 5 (4) | — (23) |
| | BC (173) | 37 (30) | 17 (13) | 42 (33) | 4 (3) | — (21) |
| 3. Environics | Atl. (140) | 48 (43) | 39 (35) | 13 (11) | 1 (1) | — (10) |
| 2–10 October | Que. (401) | 47 (43) | 23 (21) | 25 (22) | 5 (4) | — (10) |
| *(N = 1 515)* | Ont. (540) | 37 (34) | 27 (24) | 33 (30) | 3 (3) | — (10) |
| | Prairies (263) | 46 (41) | 19 (17) | 28 (25) | 8 (7) | — (10) |
| | BC (171) | 31 (27) | 22 (19) | 40 (35) | 7 (6) | — (13) |
| 5. Canadian | Atl. (315) | 45 | 38 | 14 | 2 | |
| Facts | Que. (710) | 51 | 22 | 25 | 3 | |
| 7–12 October | Ont. (685) | 33 | 32 | 33 | 3 | |
| *(N = 2 467)* | Prairies (433) | 46 | 18 | 28 | 8 | |
| | BC (324) | 41 | 17 | 40 | 3 | |
| 6. Gallup Inc. | Atl. | 44 | 33 | 22 | 0 | |
| 12–15 October | Que. | 45 | 30 | 23 | 2 | |
| *(N = 1 027)* | Ont. | 35 | 34 | 28 | 3 | |
| | Prairies | 45 | 20 | 26 | 9 | |
| | BC | 23 | 27 | 44 | 5 | |
| 8. Gallup Inc. | Atl. | 50 | 29 | 20 | 2 | |
| 20–22 October | Que. | 39 | 28 | 29 | 5 | |
| *(N = 1 034)* | Ont. | 35 | 34 | 29 | 2 | |
| | Prairies | 51 | 19 | 25 | 6 | |
| | BC | 34 | 20 | 42 | 4 | |
| 10. Angus Reid | Atl. (138) | 37 (26) | 47 (33) | 16 (11) | 0 (0) | — (29) |
| 26–27 October | Que. (392) | 43 (33) | 33 (26) | 23 (18) | 1 (1) | — (23) |
| *(N = 1 502)* | Ont. (541) | 28 (21) | 43 (32) | 28 (21) | 1 (1) | — (26) |
| | Prairies (260) | 37 (28) | 22 (17) | 34 (26) | 6 (5) | — (24) |
| | BC (171) | 35 (30) | 24 (20) | 41 (35) | 1 (1) | — (14) |
| 11. Gallup Inc. | Atl. | 32 | 43 | 23 | 2 | |
| 26–29 October | Que. | 43 | 29 | 24 | 4 | |
| *(N = 1 034)* | Ont. | 33 | 40 | 24 | 3 | |
| | Prairies | 54 | 15 | 27 | 4 | |
| | BC | 26 | 28 | 43 | 3 | |

**Table 1.9** (cont'd)
**Regional voting intentions**
(percentages)

| Polling organization, date and number of respondents | Region | Progressive Conservative | Liberal | NDP | Other | Undecided/ refused |
|---|---|---|---|---|---|---|
| 13. Environics | Atl. (67) | 35 (30) | 51 (43) | 12 (10) | 2 (2) | — (16) |
| 28–30 October | Que. (193) | 27 (22) | 42 (34) | 23 (18) | 8 (7) | — (19) |
| (N = 727) | Ont. (259) | 32 (29) | 36 (33) | 27 (25) | 5 (5) | — (9) |
| | Prairies (126) | 36 (32) | 30 (26) | 29 (25) | 5 (5) | — (12) |
| | BC (82) | 20 (19) | 33 (30) | 38 (35) | 9 (8) | — (8) |
| 14. Gallup Inc. | Atl. | 28 | 54 | 15 | 2 | |
| 2–5 November | Que. | 32 | 46 | 18 | 2 | |
| (N = 1 041) | Ont. | 28 | 49 | 20 | 3 | |
| | Prairies | 39 | 29 | 28 | 4 | |
| | BC | 33 | 28 | 32 | 7 | |
| 15. Environics | Atl. (120) | 44 (39) | 45 (39) | 10 (9) | 1 (1) | — (12) |
| 3–8 November | Que. (341) | 45 (40) | 33 (30) | 18 (16) | 4 (4) | — (10) |
| (N = 1 275) | Ont. (459) | 27 (25) | 43 (39) | 28 (26) | 3 (2) | — (8) |
| | Prairies (223) | 37 (33) | 29 (25) | 26 (23) | 9 (7) | — (11) |
| | BC (145) | 27 (24) | 32 (28) | 37 (33) | 4 (3) | — (11) |
| 16. Angus Reid | Atl. (137) | 38 (29) | 43 (32) | 18 (13) | 1 (1) | — (26) |
| 3–8 November | Que. (387) | 49 (36) | 35 (26) | 16 (12) | — (—) | — (25) |
| (N = 1 501) | Ont. (539) | 33 (26) | 41 (32) | 24 (19) | 1 (1) | — (22) |
| | Prairies (264) | 40 (32) | 24 (20) | 28 (23) | 8 (6) | — (19) |
| | BC (174) | 38 (34) | 28 (24) | 31 (27) | 3 (2) | — (13) |
| 19. Gallup Inc. | Atl. | 39 | 44 | 14 | 2 | |
| 9–12 November | Que. | 42 | 33 | 20 | 5 | |
| (N = 1 026) | Ont. | 31 | 42 | 25 | 1 | |
| | Prairies | 39 | 24 | 32 | 5 | |
| | BC | 28 | 25 | 40 | 7 | |
| 20. Gallup Inc. | Atl. | 42 | 44 | 12 | 2 | |
| 14–17 November | Que. | 47 | 32 | 17 | 4 | |
| (N = 4 067) | Ont. | 36 | 41 | 21 | 2 | |
| | Prairies | 42 | 25 | 26 | 7 | |
| | BC | 32 | 26 | 37 | 5 | |
| 21. Angus Reid | Atl. | 32 | 56 | 7 | 5 | |
| 15–17 November | Que. | 50 | 29 | 21 | 1 | |
| (N = 1 512) | Ont. | 39 | 36 | 24 | 2 | |
| | Prairies | 49 | 24 | 19 | 8 | |
| | BC | 27 | 23 | 46 | 4 | |

Table 1.9 (cont'd)
**Regional voting intentions**
(percentages)

| Polling organization, date and number of respondents | Region | Progressive Conservative | Liberal | NDP | Other | Undecided/ refused |
|---|---|---|---|---|---|---|
| Mean: all polls | Atl. | 41.3 | 42.5 | 14.6 | 1.5 | |
| | Que. | 44.0 | 31.3 | 21.7 | 3.2 | |
| | Ont. | 33.1 | 37.9 | 26.6 | 2.3 | |
| | Prairies | 44.3 | 22.9 | 26.5 | 6.5 | |
| | BC | 31.4 | 25.0 | 38.8 | 4.9 | |
| Mean: last 2 polls | Atl. | 35.0 | 50.0 | 9.5 | 3.5 | |
| | Que. | 48.5 | 30.5 | 19.0 | 2.5 | |
| | Ont. | 37.5 | 38.5 | 22.5 | 2.0 | |
| | Prairies | 45.5 | 24.5 | 22.5 | 7.5 | |
| | BC | 29.5 | 24.5 | 41.5 | 4.5 | |
| Results of 21 November 1988 election | Atl. | 41 | 46 | 11 | 2 | |
| | Que. | 53 | 30 | 14 | 3 | |
| | Ont. | 38 | 39 | 20 | 3 | |
| | Prairies | 42 | 23 | 27 | 8 | |
| | BC | 35 | 20 | 37 | 8 | |

*Notes:* N = number of respondents. The numbers in parentheses correspond to respondents' intention-to-vote before redistribution of the "undecided." Once again, the numbers may not add up to 100%.

and compared these results with those of the first Environics poll of the campaign. The table showed a loss of 18 points for the Conservatives in Manitoba. Understandably, the Conservative campaign manager in Manitoba, Terry Stratton, expressed concern that the number of respondents in Manitoba did not appear in the table ($N$ = 64 people) and that the margin of error was 12.2 percent (McFarland 1988).

This example illustrates some of the difficulties with margins of error. When a polling organization mentions the margin of error in its report, it is the "global" margin of error for the poll; in each of the categories reported on, particularly voting intentions, the margin of error will differ because the number of respondents to each question is not the same as the total number of respondents in the poll.

Comparing regional predictions of the various polls with the results of the federal election, we might expect that the figures for the less populated regions (Atlantic provinces, the Prairies and British Columbia) would show greater variations than those for Ontario or Quebec. Significant regional variations were in fact observed from one poll to another throughout the entire campaign. For example, the Conservative vote in Quebec fluctuated between 27 percent (Environics, 28–30

October) and 56 percent (Angus Reid, 2–3 October), a spread of 29 points. The Liberals received their highest score, 46 percent of voter support, in Quebec (Gallup, 2–5 November); their worst performance was 20 percent (Angus Reid, 2–3 October), a difference of 26 percentage points. The NDP reached its peak, 29 percent of the Quebec electorate, in the Gallup poll of 20–22 October, only to find itself as low as 16 percent in the Angus Reid poll of 3–8 November, a spread of 13 points. Comparable variations occurred in the other provinces.

If we look at overall results, we see that voting intentions for the Conservative party were, on average, predicted correctly in the Atlantic provinces (-0.3 percent), but the Liberal vote was underestimated by 3.5 percent and the NDP vote overestimated by 3.6 percent. In the Prairies, the Conservative vote was overestimated by 2.3 percent, and the Liberal vote was predicted correctly (-0.1 percent), as was the NDP vote (-0.5 percent). The Conservative vote in British Columbia was underestimated by 3.6 percent, the Liberal vote was overestimated by 5 percent, and the NDP vote was overestimated by 1.8 percent. In Ontario, the Conservative and Liberal votes were underestimated by 4.9 percent and 1.1 percent, respectively, whereas the NDP vote was overestimated by 6.6 percent. In Quebec, the predicted Conservative vote was 9 percent less than the real vote, the Liberal vote was 1.3 percent higher, and voting intentions for the New Democratic Party were 7.7 percent higher.

Taking into account only the last two polls of the campaign, which should normally improve accuracy, we see that regional predictions were no closer to the mark. The Conservative vote was underestimated by 6 percent in the Atlantic provinces, by 4.5 percent in Quebec, by 0.5 percent in Ontario and by 5.5 percent in British Columbia, and it was overestimated by 3.5 percent in the Prairie provinces. Liberal votes were overestimated by 4 percent in the Atlantic region, by 0.5 percent in Quebec, by 1.5 percent in the Prairies and by 4.5 percent in British Columbia, but they were underestimated by 0.5 percent in Ontario. As for the New Democratic Party, its strength was underestimated by 1.5 percent in the Atlantic region and by 4.5 percent in the Prairies but overestimated by 5 percent in Quebec, by 2.5 percent in Ontario and by 4.5 percent in British Columbia.

This analysis shows that any attempt to predict the regional vote from Canada-wide survey data is subject to considerable risk. The potential for error is so great that the question is really whether the game is worth the candle, even though the predictions are correct in a general way – that is, they fall within the margins of error but not necessarily the global margin of error usually published. Why, then, do pollsters agree to the publication of these results in the newspapers?

Michael Adams says that pollsters are under great pressure, partly from the regional media, to publish these results: "Environics is caught in a dilemma. We get a tremendous pressure to give individual numbers for the Western provinces, a tremendous amount of pressure" (McFarland 1988). In the final analysis, however, pollsters make their regional results public despite these difficulties; as a result, the public may be misled about the nature and extent of variations within a region and relative to other regions.

### Predicting the Number of Seats

Gallup is the only polling organization in Canada that ventures to predict the number of seats that will be held by the major parties after an election. As table 1.10 shows, Gallup's overall figures underestimated Conservative seats by 10, overestimated Liberal seats by 14 and underestimated NDP seats by 4. Looking at the last poll of the campaign, the predictions were only slightly more accurate for the Conservatives, at 7 seats fewer than they actually won; no more accurate for the Liberals, at 14 seats more; and less accurate for the NDP, at 7 seats fewer. In the case of the Liberals, the best estimate was that of the first poll, which predicted 82 seats.

Translating voting intentions into numbers of seats is not easy, particularly in the Canadian context with its many regional variations and three-party races. Although Gallup consistently refuses to reveal

**Table 1.10**
**Gallup Inc.'s predictions of number of seats**

|  | Progressive Conservative | Liberal | NDP | Total |
|---|---|---|---|---|
| 1. 1–2 October | 186 | 82 | 27 | 295 |
| 2. 12–15 October | 183 | 64 | 48 | 295 |
| 3. 20–22 October | 193 | 56 | 46 | 295 |
| 4. 26–29 October | 154 | 102 | 39 | 295 |
| 5. 2–5 November | 91 | 170 | 34 | 295 |
| 6. 9–12 November | 141 | 112 | 42 | 295 |
| 7. 14–17 November | 162 | 97 | 36 | 295 |
| Mean: Gallup's predictions | 159 | 97 | 39 | 295 |
| Kay's predictions | 174 | 78 | 43 | 295 |
| 1988 election results | 169 | 83 | 43 | 295 |

its method of predicting seats, claiming that this procedure is a trade secret, it is obvious that the procedure is based on the famous cube law, which was revealed in 1909 to the British Royal Commission on Electoral Systems by the Englishman James Parker Smith (Lakeman 1974, 78; Boursin 1990, 158–60). The cube law stipulates that in a bipartisan system the number of seats is a function of the popular vote and is calculated as the ratio between the cube of the proportion of the popular vote received by each party:

$$\text{Ratio of } N \text{ seats} \quad = \quad \frac{(\% \text{ of vote to party A})^3}{(\% \text{ of vote to party B})^3}$$

For example, if party A receives 60 percent of the vote and party B receives 40 percent, the seats will be distributed in the ratio of $60^3/40^3$ = 3.37. If there are 295 seats, party A will receive 3.37 times the seats of party B, that is, about 227 seats (77 percent) versus 68 (23 percent) for party B.

In the Canadian electoral system, however, where there are more than two parties, the cube law cannot be directly applied without some modifications (Qualter 1968; Spafford 1970). Among the various methods proposed, the one that appears to come closest to Gallup's is, according to Lorne Bozinoff, vice-president of Gallup Canada Inc., the model proposed by Barry J. Kay (1990). Kay proposes a "regional cube law" in which one applies this law to each region (Atlantic, Quebec, Ontario, Prairies, British Columbia) while taking into account specific characteristics of each, particularly (1) the changes that occurred in the actual vote for each party in the various constituencies in relation to the previous election (assuming the local vote will follow the regional trend), and (2) whether a riding is being defended by the incumbent. Taking these two variables into account, Kay made very accurate predictions for the 1988 election: the Conservative seats were overestimated by only five, the Liberal seats were underestimated by five, and the NDP seats were predicted correctly.

Kay used electoral data to develop his model; it is only one step from there to using pollsters' predictions of voting intentions. It would appear that Gallup's model is based on this concept of change in the regional vote. Gallup's commercial interest in protecting its process is understandable, but we must remember that it is based on survey data on voting intentions; confidence in the validity of the survey results is a prerequisite for using them to predict the number of seats. As table 1.10 shows, there were significant gaps between the predicted number of seats and the actual number obtained by each party on election night. Without doubt this type of information has a public relations impact, especially when the media repeat it, but does it not undermine confidence in the accuracy of polls? Pollsters and the public in France treat such information with great mistrust, because the peculiarities of the French electoral system make it almost impossible to predict accurately who will win the majority of seats in legislative elections.

## CONFIDENTIALITY OF INFORMATION ABOUT RESPONDENTS

Of all the information missing from polling reports, among the most serious gaps is the polling organizations' failure to specify what measures they take to protect the confidentiality of information about respondents. In all scientific research, the Canada Council, university researchers and organizations dedicated to the protection of civil liberties insist on this point: it is essential that the confidentiality of information gathered in any poll be preserved and that no one be able to trace the identity of respondents.

The polling reports contain no information that could lead to identification of respondents. However, none of the reports specifies for how long or in what form survey data are stored. Do interviewers inform respondents of their right to refuse to answer certain questions? Do they specify that the information gathered will remain confidential? How do they obtain the consent of interviewees? At the end of interviews, do they tell respondents that they can call a certain telephone number and receive a copy of the survey in which they participated? In our view, every polling organization should meet these requirements, no matter what the cost, and every research report should clearly identify the decisions and actions taken to meet these research requirements.

## CONCLUSION

In summary, our review of survey reports by Canadian polling organizations reveals that despite the existence of standards of practice and codes of ethics, certain elements are missing from published results. These gaps could be filled with relative ease and the quality of reports improved if the organizations looked beyond the constraints of the media. Gallup's report, for example, contains only a brief description of the methodology and a descriptive presentation of results; in short, the report provides little more than the information broadcast by the media.

The other organizations, Canadian Facts and Angus Reid, do not fare much better, although their reports do provide more cross-tabulations. The fact that Environics researchers wrote the newspaper articles on their polls in the *Globe and Mail* (and their report is essentially a summary of the articles, to which they have added some tables) is evidence of the difficulties of finding journalists qualified to provide rigorous analysis of polls results. Surely there are some journalists in Canada capable of conveying the subtleties of poll methodology, and surely there is training that could help others attain this knowledge. The credibility of the polling organizations is further reduced when no statistical measures (e.g., coefficients of correlation, degree of significance of relationships) are presented and when results are presented in rounded whole numbers.

Polling organizations should make greater efforts to improve the presentation and the technical quality of their reports. At present, descriptions of methodology are inadequate and do not conform to the rules established by the profession. Without this information, it is impossible for the public to assess the integrity of pollsters and the validity of their results, even if they do have access to survey reports. How can one obtain technical information if polling organizations fail to abide by the criteria and standards they themselves have established? Is regulation the only way to ensure public access to technical information?

In some cases no survey report exists; instead, the organization prepares a very brief document presenting the main results of interest to journalists. This is why, in France, the notice sent by the organizations to the polling commission contains only technical information, often only one page long. The commission may, however, request more detailed information, as it often does. Even access to this type of information would be a major step and would require only a modest effort on the part of polling organizations. There may always be some who refuse to make this information available; this could lead governments to regulate to ensure a certain uniformity of behaviour.

# 7

# THE JOURNALISTIC TREATMENT OF POLLS DURING THE 1988 FEDERAL ELECTION CAMPAIGN

Hᴏᴡ ᴊᴏᴜʀɴᴀʟɪsᴛs ᴛʀᴇᴀᴛ polls during an election campaign is an issue of some importance to those who argue that polls serve only the commercial interests of the media. Be that as it may, survey reports from polling organizations are not particularly informative and leave room for much interpretation. Should journalists be expected to examine this information with a magnifying glass and analyse its every detail? Should survey specifications sheets be prepared in a manner that makes them readily accessible to the public?

In their analysis of the 1984 election, Alan Frizzell and Anthony Westell reviewed how seven Canadian newspapers (the *Vancouver Sun*, *Winnipeg Free Press*, the *Globe and Mail*, *Toronto Star*, Montreal *Gazette*, *La Presse*, Halifax *Chronicle-Herald*) had covered the polls (Frizzell and Westell 1985). Among other things, they observed that newspapers in Canada tended to present voting intentions only, and also gave an impression of the election as a horse race. They noted some improvement in the provision of survey specifications, but only one article in four included complete methodological information. Using the same approach for the 1988 election, Frizzell (1989, 98) found that the situation had deteriorated overall: not one newspaper article followed the guidelines of the Canadian Daily Newspaper Publishers Association on poll reporting. The newspaper with the

best record overall was the *Globe and Mail,* no doubt because its articles were written by the pollsters.

We analysed the content of all articles on polls published in the
Canadian press during the 1988 election, applying the criteria suggested
by the Regroupement québécois des sciences sociales. Initially, we examined only the articles published by the sponsor of a poll, that is, the
journalistic coverage of the poll when it first appeared in the newspaper or newspapers that commissioned the survey. We also looked
for any indications of cross-referencing or paraphrasing, that is, articles about the poll published after its first publication or broadcast,
whether in the original paper or in another newspaper (Beaud 1989).
We did not conduct a systematic analysis of all the articles, although we
compiled about 100, but a straight reading of them was sufficient to
identify the problems with them: in general, they provided even less
methodological information than the original articles. We started with
coverage in the written press of polls carried out by Insight Canada
Research/CTV and Canadian Facts/CBC; we considered them cross-
referenced because the primary source was the broadcaster.

Gallup and other polls may be conducted for one sponsor or for a
group of subscribers. All the Angus Reid polls were done for the Southam
News chain: one poll would make the headlines on the same day in
various dailies, for example, *Le Soleil,* the *Gazette,* the *Ottawa Citizen.* We
therefore compared the journalistic treatment of these polls. In the case
of Environics, there was only one sponsor, the *Globe and Mail.*

We had no information on radio broadcasts of poll results. We were
unable to find a source of tapes or transcripts of radio news reports,
which would have permitted a more complete analysis of this medium.
Nevertheless, we believe that our observations about television news
treatment of polls also apply to radio.

### IDENTITY OF THE POLLING ORGANIZATION, SPONSOR, INTERVIEW PERIOD AND COLLECTION METHOD

The first criterion was the name of the organization conducting the survey;
it was mentioned in every case (see table 1.11). Gallup Inc. was the most
active, conducting seven polls; Insight Canada Research conducted five;
Environics and Angus Reid, four each; and Canadian Facts, two.

The second criterion was sponsorship: the print media remain the
principal clients of polling organizations. The *Globe and Mail* is associated with Environics; Southam News with Angus Reid; and the *Toronto
Star* with Gallup. The *Star* advised its readers, after publishing the
results of the first poll of the campaign, that it intended to concentrate
on Gallup polls so that polls did not push issues off the pages of the daily:

**Table 1.11**
**Specifications sheet of cross-Canada polls as published in print media during the 1988 federal election campaign**

| Organization and interview date | Sponsor | Collection method | Initial sample | Ineligible | Rejection rate | Respondents | Response rate | Margin of error | Weighting variables | Sampling method |
|---|---|---|---|---|---|---|---|---|---|---|
| 1. Gallup Inc. 1–2 October | Toronto Star | Telephone | n.a. | n.a. | n.a. | 1 061 | n.a. | 4.0 | n.a. | n.a. |
| 2. Angus Reid 3–4 October | Southam News | Telephone | n.a. | n.a. | n.a. | 1 512 | n.a. | 2.5 | n.a. | n.a. |
| 3. Environics 2–10 October | Globe and Mail | Telephone | n.a. | n.a. | n.a. | 1 515 | n.a. | 2.5 | n.a. | Multi-stage stratified |
| 4. Insight Canada Research 6–13 October | CTV | Telephone | n.a. | n.a. | n.a. | 1 100 | n.a. | 3.2 | n.a. | n.a. |
| 5. Canadian Facts 7–12 October | CBC/Radio-Canada | Telephone | n.a. | n.a. | n.a. | 2 467 | n.a. | 2.1 | n.a. | n.a. |
| 6. Gallup Inc. 12–15 October | Subscribers | Face-to-face | n.a. | n.a. | n.a. | 1 027 | n.a. | 4.0 | n.a. | n.a. |
| 7. Insight Canada Research 13–20 October | CTV | Telephone | n.a. | n.a. | n.a. | 1 100 | n.a. | 3.2 | n.a. | n.a. |
| 8. Gallup Inc. 20–22 October | Toronto Star | Telephone | n.a. | n.a. | n.a. | 1 034 | n.a. | 4.0 | n.a. | n.a. |

**Table 1.11 (cont'd)**
**Specifications sheet of cross-Canada polls as published in print media during the 1988 federal election campaign**

| Organization and interview date | Sponsor | Collection method | Initial sample | Ineligible | Rejection rate | Respondents | Response rate | Margin of error | Weighting variables | Sampling method |
|---|---|---|---|---|---|---|---|---|---|---|
| 9. Environics 25–26 October | Globe and Mail | Telephone | n.a. | n.a. | n.a. | 811 | n.a. | 3.4 | n.a. | Multi-stage stratified |
| 10. Angus Reid 26–27 October | Southam News | Telephone | n.a. | n.a. | n.a. | 1 502 | n.a. | 2.5 | n.a. | n.a. |
| 11. Gallup Inc. 26–29 October | Subscribers | Face-to-face | n.a. | n.a. | n.a. | 1 034 | n.a. | 4.0 | n.a. | n.a. |
| 12. Insight Canada Research 27–30 October | CTV | Telephone | n.a. | n.a. | n.a. | n.a. | n.a. | 3.2 | n.a. | n.a. |
| 13. Environics 28–30 October | Globe and Mail | Telephone | n.a. | n.a. | n.a. | 727 | n.a. | 3.6 | n.a. | Multi-stage stratified |
| 14. Gallup Inc. 2–5 November | Subscribers | Face-to-face | n.a. | n.a. | n.a. | 1 041 | n.a. | 4.0 | n.a. | n.a. |
| 15. Environics 3–8 November | Globe and Mail | Telephone | 1 745 | n.a. | n.a. | 1 275 | 73 | 2.7 | n.a. | Multi-stage stratified/ focus group |
| 16. Angus Reid 3–8 November | Southam News | Telephone | n.a. | n.a. | n.a. | 1 501 | n.a. | 2.5 | Age, sex | n.a. |

**Table 1.11** (cont'c)
**Specifications sheet of cross-Canada polls as published in print media during the 1988 federal election campaign**

| Organization and interview date | Sponsor | Collection method | Initial sample | Ineligible | Rejection rate | Respondents | Response rate | Margin of error | Weighting variables | Sampling method |
|---|---|---|---|---|---|---|---|---|---|---|
| 17. Insight Canada Research 3–10 November | CTV | Telephone | n.a. | n.a. | n.a. | 1 120 | n.a. | 3.2 | n.a. | n.a. |
| 18. Canadian Facts 5–8 November | CBC/ "The National" | Telephone | n.a. | n.a. | n.a. | 2 200 | n.a. | 2.2 | n.a. | n.a. |
| 19. Gallup Inc. 9–12 November | *Toronto Star* | Face-to-face | n.a. | n.a. | n.a. | 1 026 | n.a. | 4.0 | n.a. | n.a. |
| 20. Gallup Inc. 14–17 November | *Toronto Star* *La Presse* | Face-to-face, telephone | n.a. | n.a. | n.a. | 2 097 1 970 | n.a. | 3.0 | n.a. | n.a. |
| 21. Angus Reid 15–17 November | Southam News | Telephone | n.a. | n.a. | n.a. | 1 512 | n.a. | 2.5 | Age, sex | n.a. |
| 22. Insight Canada Research not available | CTV | Telephone | n.a. | n.a. | n.a. | 2 700 | n.a. | n.a. | n.a. | n.a. |

*Note:* n.a. = not available.

"During the current election campaign the *Star* will feature polls conducted by Gallup, a highly respected and independent polling agency. The *Star* will report on other polls as they appear, but will not give them the same prominence. Our intention is not to drown readers in public opinion surveys at the expense of a discussion on the issues in the campaign" (*Toronto Star* 1988).

Fifteen of the 22 polls of the campaign were sponsored by the print media. Two broadcasters either sponsored or conducted polls during the election campaign: CTV and CBC/Radio-Canada. The CTV network was the more active, collaborating with Insight Canada Research to broadcast the results of five polls; CBC/Radio-Canada sponsored only two polls, conducted by Canadian Facts. Since the policy of CBC/Radio-Canada is not to broadcast their own polls during the last 10 days of an election campaign, CTV had a clear field and was the only broadcaster to present its own polls during the campaign's final days.[10]

The third criterion was interview period: the timeframe for the interviews was specified in most cases. However, for the last poll of the campaign, broadcast on Saturday 19 November, two days before the election, the dates of the interviews were not mentioned. In addition, the somewhat fragmentary results of this poll by Insight Canada Research were published in the newspapers on the eve of the election. This appears to have been an isolated incident. Can citizens not expect a higher standard of behaviour on the part of the newspapers, even though the 48-hour rule does not apply to the print media? How could even moderately perspicacious citizens be expected to react and exercise their right of rejoinder? Given the amount of time left, this right was rendered ineffective.

The last criterion was collection method: data-collection methods were reported correctly, although with some variations. Only Gallup opted for face-to-face interviews (four polls), telephone interviews (two polls), and, in one case, a poll combining both methods. In this case, as in preceding polls, the reader required a certain attentiveness to recognize that Gallup's methodology varied from one poll to the next, although the articles did contain this information.

### INITIAL SAMPLE, INELIGIBLE RESPONDENTS AND SAMPLING METHOD
In describing methodology, no newspaper mentioned the number of respondents rejected from a sample or the reasons for their exclusion; no rejection rate was reported for any of the polls. Only the final Environics poll stated the size of the initial sample: this was the second part of a two-stage panel survey, so the figure was the same as the final sample of the first Environics poll of the campaign. These were

the same shortcomings that we observed earlier in the reports from polling organizations.

With respect to sampling methods, we also observed that the press tended to provide relatively few details. In the Gallup polls, for example, no mention was made of the sampling approach: Was the quota method used? Random selection? Stratification techniques? The fact that Gallup used both face-to-face and telephone interviews makes it more difficult for the elector to grasp all these nuances.

The description of the sampling methods used by the other polling organizations was also absent. Only Environics provided a relatively complete presentation of methodology. However, in the poll made public by this firm on 1 November, readers learned the total number of respondents was the sum of those who answered between 25 and 26 October and between 28 and 30 October. There is no indication, however, whether the people contacted were selected from different samples or whether both groups were from one sample. Grouping the results of two polls and differentiating them in the tables could lead readers to believe that only one sample was involved.

Finally, the sample for the Environics poll of 3 to 8 November was composed of respondents from the first Environics poll of the campaign, conducted between 2 and 10 October. The number of respondents in the first poll was 1 515; the final sample was 1 745 respondents. Environics must have called all these people again, but this time, only 1 275 responded. It would, therefore, have been more appropriate to speak of a survey conducted in two successive stages, one at the beginning of October and one at the beginning of November.

## NUMBER OF RESPONDENTS AND RESPONSE RATE

The only information given regularly and consistently in the written press was the number of respondents. Most Canada-wide polls start with initial samples high enough to produce 1 000 respondents by the end of the survey. Only Environics was below this number in two of its four polls. Obviously, the number of respondents does not guarantee the quality of a poll or its journalistic presentation. Nevertheless, it appears that $N = 1\ 000$ is becoming the standard for the profession, especially for Canada-wide polls.

The response rate, however, was consistently absent from newspaper articles, except for the Environics survey at the beginning of November, which stipulated a response rate of 73 percent. Yet, calculating the response rate is relatively straightforward. The response rate is simply the percentage of respondents in (not excluded from) the final sample who agreed to answer all the questions. It would no doubt be more accurate to speak of the participation rate, as the Quebec firm

CROP does, but the expression "response rate" has become common. This information is essential in assessing the extent of a polling organization's efforts to contact the greatest possible number of people for its final sample. Some pollsters call more than four times to contact the person selected. The nature of response rates remains one of the great mysteries in the journalistic treatment of pre-election polls in the 1988 campaign.

### MARGINS OF ERROR, WEIGHTING AND ADJUSTMENT

We can see from table 1.11 that margins of error were presented for all polls made public during the 1988 election, with the exception of the last poll by Insight Canada Research. As we pointed out earlier, there are significant differences in how these figures are presented, and in many cases they are, to put it bluntly, inaccurate.

Only two of the polls, both by Angus Reid, were accompanied by a description of the weighting variables applied to the results. Surprisingly, however, there was no indication of whether results were adjusted on a national, regional or local basis; nor were the most important variables, such as language, mentioned.

### HEADLINES, SIGNATURES, PRESENTATION OF QUESTIONS AND METHODOLOGY

Four other factors relate less to methodology than to the way poll results are presented: the relevance of the headlines, the signatures on the articles, the presentation of the questions and the use of an insert detailing methodology.

In 1979, the joint polling committee of the Canadian Political Science Association and the Canadian Association of French-Speaking Sociologists and Anthropologists (which would become the Regroupement québécois des sciences sociales in 1983) recommended that journalists pay particular attention when giving titles to polls so that "the headlines and the titles of articles on polls highlight only the most reliable data; these data must, of course, be detailed in tables to permit readers to judge the quality of the sample, the questions and the interpretation of the data" (Comité des sondages 1979, 24). No one needs to be reminded of cases where headlines did not correspond to poll results (V. Lemieux 1988, 63–64). We paid particular attention to the headlines of certain newspapers (*Toronto Star*, *Le Soleil*, Montreal *Gazette*, *Ottawa Citizen*, *La Presse*) during the 1988 federal campaign to determine how they had referred to various polls on the day of publication. These titles, along with other information about the published articles, are given in table 1.12. On the whole, these dailies accurately reflected the polling data in their headlines.

**Table 1.12**
**Journalistic treatment of polls: headline, byline, questions asked, use of methodological insert**

| Polling organization/ interview dates | Newspaper | Date of publication | Headline | Byline | Questions | Insert |
|---|---|---|---|---|---|---|
| 1. Gallup Inc. 1–2 October | *Toronto Star* | 3 October | Tories top poll at 43%, trade seen as key issue | No | Yes | No |
| 2. Angus Reid 3–4 October | *Le Soleil* | 5 October | Le PC est encore plus fort au pays | Yes | Yes | No |
| | *The Gazette* | 5 October | Poll gives Tories 45%, NDP 27, Liberals 26 | Yes | No | No |
| | *Ottawa Citizen* | 5 October | PCs build 18-point lead in poll | No | No | No |
| 3. Environics 2–10 October | *Globe and Mail* | 12 October | Tories jump to wide lead in poll as NDP bumps Liberals to third | Yes | Yes | Yes |
| 6. Gallup Inc. 12–15 October | *La Presse* | 17 October | Le PC perd du terrain, selon Gallup | Yes | No | No |
| | *Le Soleil* | 17 October | Le NPD grimpe de six points aux dépens des autres partis | Yes | Yes | No |
| | *The Gazette* | 17 October | Poll finds PCs slip lower but still lead by 10 points | No | No | No |
| 8. Gallup Inc. 20–22 October | *Toronto Star* | 24 October | Tories keep their big lead Gallup finds | Yes | No | No |
| 9. Environics 25–26 October | *Globe and Mail* | 28 October | Turner won debates, survey says | Yes | Yes | Yes |
| 10. Angus Reid 26–27 October | *The Gazette* | 29 October | Liberals, Tories in dead heat: poll | Yes | No | No |
| | *Ottawa Citizen* | 29 October | Born-again Grits catch Tories | Yes | No | No |

**Table 1.12** (cont'd)
**Journalistic treatment of polls: headline, byline, questions asked, use of methodological insert**

| Polling organization/ interview dates | Newspaper | Date of publication | Headline | Byline | Questions | Insert |
|---|---|---|---|---|---|---|
| 11. Gallup Inc. 26–29 October | Toronto Star | 31 October | Liberals close gap in latest Gallup | Yes | Yes | No |
| | The Gazette | 31 October | Gallup finds Liberals gain, but PCs keep lead | No | No | No |
| | La Presse | 31 October | Gallup: PC 38%, PLC 32%, NPD 27% | Yes | No | No |
| | Le Soleil | 31 October | Le PC reste seul en tête | Yes | Yes | No |
| 13. Environics 28–30 October | Globe and Mail | 1 November | Liberals move ahead of PCs in wake of leaders debates | Yes | Yes | Yes |
| 14. Gallup Inc. 2–5 November | The Gazette | 7 November | Gallup finds Liberals soar to 43% | No | No | No |
| | Le Soleil | 7 November | Bonne mais fragile avance des libéraux | Yes | Yes | No |
| | La Presse | 7 November | Les conservateurs en chute libre – Gallup : PLC 43%, PC 31%, NPD 22% | Yes | No | No |
| 15. Environics 3–8 November | Globe and Mail | 10 November | Tories and Liberals are neck-and-neck, new survey shows | Yes | Yes | Yes |
| 16. Angus Reid 3–8 November | Le Soleil | 10 November | Le PC reprend le premier rang | Yes | Yes | No |
| | Ottawa Citizen | 10 November | Tories bounce back, poll shows | No | No | No |
| | The Gazette | 10 November | Reid poll gives Tories 39%, Liberals 35% | No | No | No |
| | La Presse | 10 November | Les conservateurs remontent la pente | Yes | No | No |

Table 1.12 (cont'd)
**Journalistic treatment of polls: headline, byline, questions asked, use of methodological insert**

| Polling organization/ interview dates | Newspaper | Date of publication | Headline | Byline | Questions | Insert |
|---|---|---|---|---|---|---|
| 19. Gallup Inc. 9–12 November | *Toronto Star* | 14 November | Liberals tie with Tories, says Gallup | Yes | Yes | No |
| 20. Gallup Inc. 14–17 November | *Toronto Star* | 19 November | Tories headed for majority, Gallup says | Yes | Yes | No |
|  | *La Presse* | 19 November | Les "bleus" font des gains | Yes | No | No |
| 21. Angus Reid 15–17 November | *Ottawa Citizen* | 19 November | Tories grab eight-point lead in poll | Yes | No | No |
|  | *The Gazette* | 19 November | Final polls put Tories ahead | No | No | No |
|  | *Le Soleil* | 19 November | Les conservateurs s'acheminent vers un gouvernement majoritaire | Yes | No | No |
| Total | | | | 23/31 | 13/31 | 4/31 |
| Percentages | | | | 74.2 | 41.9 | 12.9 |

Twenty-three of the 31 articles (74.2 percent) carried a signature. Sometimes, articles appearing in two different dailies were signed by the same Canadian Press journalist. The *Gazette* only signed two articles out of seven. With the exception of this newspaper, the dailies provided this information for the most part.

In only 13 of 31 articles (41.9 percent) did we find the wording of the question on voting intentions reflected in the headline. Only one daily achieved a perfect score, the *Globe and Mail* (all four of its published articles), followed by *Le Soleil* (five out of six). In the first case, the question on voting intentions was found in the methodological insert accompanying poll results. In the second case, it was in the tables illustrating the evolution of the electors' voting intentions; the exception was the last poll of the campaign, published on 19 November. Once again, this information did not appear in any article published in the *Gazette*.

Methodological inserts, that is, spaces reserved for methodological information about polls, were not used in any daily other than the *Globe and Mail*, which published the Environics polls. Once again, only one newspaper obtained a perfect score: all articles were signed, questions about intentions to vote were pinpointed, and the methodology was adequately presented. Like Alan Frizzell, we observed that coverage of polls by the *Globe and Mail* was superior to coverage by other dailies; this was no doubt because the articles and graphic presentation of the polls were supplied by the same firm that conducted the polls. Can we conclude that pollsters, who are well aware of the limitations of their measurement tools, would prefer that journalists give more emphasis to the methodological aspects of their polls? Our analysis tends to confirm this hypothesis.

## GRAPHIC PRESENTATION

The Comité des sondages underlined, in 1979, the importance of the graphic presentation of polls in the media and asked the media to give special attention to the tables. Each table, and in particular those on voting intentions, must be accompanied by five elements:

   i.  the exact wording of the questions, as well as the translation used in the case of a poll conducted with more than one linguistic group;

  ii.  the number of respondents upon which the percentages in each column or category are based;

 iii. the percentage of respondents who did not answer a particular question;

 iv. the percentages based on the total number of respondents in each column or category, including those who did not answer; and

  v. the classification of categories of respondents. (Comité des sondages 1979, 24)

The dailies never present the wording of questions in both official languages, and rarely is the wording of the question on voting intentions found on the chart or table presenting the results on this question. How can readers determine whether the question on voting intentions was worded in a neutral manner? Gallup's question, for example, is rendered in extraordinarily clumsy French. Poor translation of questions on voting intentions is, in fact, quite common. Two dailies did, however, include the wording of the question on voting intentions in their tables during the 1988 election campaign; they were *Le Soleil* (1988) and the *Toronto Star* (figure 1.1).

The absolute number of respondents in each category is always missing from the tables accompanying poll results. This element is essential, particularly when the pollsters go on to make regional projections, as Gallup and Environics did. As figures 1.1 and 1.2 demonstrate, because these regional percentages are missing, each region appears to be of similar significance in the overall sample, and the numbers who did not answer one question or another are not shown at all. These respondents were excluded from tables, yet the percentages presented were calculated on 100 percent; but more often than not, the sum of the percentages is not 100. Furthermore, there is not always a note at the bottom of the tables to inform readers that the figures may not add to 100 percent because of rounding.

The presentation of the regional results suffers greatly because of these basic mistakes. When the number of respondents per region is not indicated, regional voters have reason to be frustrated; presenting results in this way gives a false picture of public opinion and makes it impossible to judge the reliability of the results. After the many criticisms it received from Manitoba, Environics decided to indicate, in the methodological insert for its last poll of the campaign, the number of respondents per region and the regional margins of error; it also included a note below the table to the effect that margins of error vary between regions (see figure 1.2). Of course, these steps would have been unnecessary if the five rules for presenting tables had been consistently followed.

Another important fact that should be present in the tables is a breakdown of the various categories of respondents. The lack of this information is particularly evident in the case of voting intentions, where the number of people choosing to abstain or spoil their ballot is never indicated, despite the fact that some voters do make this choice. Why are these voters completely absent from the tables? Do they exist? Polling organizations should distinguish these categories, as well as "don't know" and "refuse to answer."

**Figure 1.1**
**Results of a Gallup poll published in the *Toronto Star***

| GALLUP POLL | | | | |
|---|---|---|---|---|
| Which party's candidate will you be most likely to support in Monday's election? | | | | |
| | PC | Lib. | NDP | Other |
| Canada | 40% | 35% | 22% | 3% |
| Regional breakdown: | | | | |
| Atlantic | 42 | 44 | 12 | 2 |
| Quebec | 47 | 32 | 17 | 4 |
| ONTARIO | 36 | 41 | 21 | 2 |
| Prairies | 42 | 25 | 26 | 7 |
| B.C. | 32 | 26 | 37 | 5 |
| If a federal election were held today, which party's candidate do you think you would favor? | | | | |
| By income: | | | | |
| Under $20,000 | 37 | 36 | 23 | 4 |
| $20,000–$29,999 | 36 | 37 | 23 | 3 |
| $30,000–$39,999 | 39 | 34 | 23 | 4 |
| $40,000+ | 46 | 33 | 19 | 3 |
| Best prime minister | | | | |
| Who would make the best prime minister? | | | | |
| Mulroney | Turner | Broadbent | None | Don't know |
| 33 | 17 | 24 | 14 | 13 |
| Free trade | | | | |
| Whom do you believe on free trade? | | | | |
| Mulroney | Turner | Broadbent | None | Don't know |
| 36 | 19 | 13 | 14 | 19 |
| Are you in favor of the proposed free trade agreement with the United States? | | | | |
| | Favor | Oppose | Neither | Don't know |
| Nov. 14–17 | 34 | 41 | 7 | 18 |
| Regional breakdown: | | | | |
| Atlantic | 27 | 46 | 1 | 26 |
| Quebec | 41 | 27 | 15 | 17 |
| ONTARIO | 30 | 49 | 4 | 17 |
| Prairies | 35 | 42 | 4 | 19 |
| B.C. | 32 | 48 | 3 | 17 |

*Source: Toronto Star,* 19 November 1988.

*Note:* Percentages may not add up to 100 due to rounding.

The scale of graphic presentations is also important and can create different impressions of the evolution of voting intentions depending on one's paper. For example, we compared three graphs published on 10 November 1988 in *Le Soleil* (Forgues 1988), the Montreal *Gazette* (1988) and the *Ottawa Citizen* (1988); all three presented the results of Angus Reid's poll of 3 to 8 November. The graphs were run on the front pages of all three newspapers. Voting intentions, expressed as percentages, were depicted on the *y* axis; the *x* axis showed various dates during the campaign. The graphs differed both in scale and in the dates used. The *Ottawa Citizen* tracked 18 polls on its graph; *Le Soleil* and the *Gazette* depicted 10 each, though not the same polls.

Because of its scale and dimensions, the graph in the *Gazette* gave the impression of a much tighter race than shown by the graphs presented in the *Ottawa Citizen* and *Le Soleil*. Moreover, the gap separating the Progressive Conservatives and the Liberals in the last Angus Reid poll was depicted as being much narrower than in the other two newspapers. These differences are surprising, given that the graphs were based on the same poll. It would be to the advantage of polling organizations to supply the graphs that should accompany poll results. This would at least ensure that the graphic representation of polls did not differ from one newspaper to another.

Finally, the winner of the "worst graphic" award for the 1988 federal campaign goes to the *Montreal Daily News* for its representation of an Insight Canada poll conducted on 27 and 30 October (Black 1988). Not only does the graph have no title, but the scale is clearly inaccurate; readers cannot tell at a glance which line corresponds to which political party. These difficulties were compounded by a printing problem; an attempt was made to indicate the phenomenal rise of the Liberal party, but the resulting arrow was barely legible. Nor is there any

**Figure 1.2**
**Technical information reported with poll published in the *Globe and Mail***

|  | National | | Atlantic | | Quebec | | Montreal | | Outside Montreal | |
|---|---|---|---|---|---|---|---|---|---|---|
|  | Oct. 2–10 | Nov. 3–8 | Oct. 2–10 | Nov. 3–8 | Oct. 2–10 | Nov. 3–8 | Oct. 2–10 | Nov. 3–8 | Oct. 2–10 | Nov. 3–8 |
| PC | 42 | 35 | 48 | 44 | 47 | 45 | 41 | 40 | 53 | 49 |
| Liberal | 25 | 37 | 39 | 45 | 23 | 33 | 25 | 30 | 22 | 31 |
| NDP | 29 | 24 | 13 | 10 | 25 | 18 | 28 | 19 | 21 | 16 |
| Other | 5 | 5 | 1 | 1 | 5 | 4 | 6 | 5 | 4 | 4 |

**Figure 1.2** (cont'd)
## Technical information reported with poll published in the *Globe and Mail*

|  | Ontario | | Toronto | | Outside Toronto | |
|---|---|---|---|---|---|---|
|  | Oct. 2–10 | Nov. 3–8 | Oct. 2–10 | Nov. 3–8 | Oct. 2–10 | Nov. 3–8 |
| PC | 37 | 27 | 38 | 31 | 37 | 25 |
| Liberal | 27 | 43 | 26 | 43 | 27 | 43 |
| NDP | 33 | 28 | 33 | 24 | 33 | 29 |
| Other | 3 | 3 | 3 | 2 | 3 | 3 |

|  | The West | | Manitoba | | Saskatchewan | | Alberta | | British Columbia | |
|---|---|---|---|---|---|---|---|---|---|---|
|  | Oct. 2–10 | Nov. 3–8 | Oct. 2–10 | Nov. 3–8 | Oct. 2–10 | Nov. 3–8 | Oct. 2–10 | Nov. 3–8 | Oct. 2–10 | Nov. 3–8 |
| PC | 40 | 34 | 48 | 33 | 41 | 37 | 49 | 42 | 31 | 27 |
| Liberal | 19 | 29 | 32 | 46 | 10 | 18 | 15 | 23 | 22 | 32 |
| NDP | 32 | 28 | 16 | 18 | 44 | 44 | 24 | 16 | 40 | 37 |
| Other | 8 | 8 | 5 | 4 | 6 | 2 | 12 | 19 | 7 | 4 |

Margins of error differ in various regions. Bernard Bennell, *Globe and Mail.*

| Region | Number of respondents | Margin of error (%) |
|---|---|---|
| Atlantic | 123 | ± 8.8 |
| Quebec | 314 | ± 5.5 |
| Ontario | 460 | ± 4.6 |
| Manitoba | 61 | ±12.5 |
| Saskatchewan | 53 | ±13.5 |
| Alberta | 120 | ± 8.9 |
| B.C. | 144 | ± 8.2 |

## Methodology

The results of today's poll for *The Globe and Mail* by Environics Research Group Ltd. are based on interviews with a representative nationwide sample of 1 275 eligible voters. The interviews were conducted between Nov. 3 and Nov. 8 in English and French.

Interviewing was conducted from Environics' office in Toronto.

The margin of error for a sample of 1 275 is plus or minus 2.7 percentage points in 19 out of 20 samples.

The regional distribution of respondents and the corresponding margins of error in 19 out of 20 samples are outlined in the accompanying table.

All respondents in today's poll originally had been interviewed as part of the Globe-Environics Poll conducted Oct. 2 to Oct. 10 and reported in *The Globe* Oct. 12 to Oct. 15. By returning to these

Figure 1.2 (cont'd)
**Technical information reported with poll published in the *Globe and Mail***

respondents, the pollsters were able to track changes in voting intentions over the past four weeks and determine the effect of significant events during the election campaign on individual voters.

Of the 1 745 respondents interviewed in early October, 73 per cent subsequently were contacted again and interviewed for the new poll.

Respondents were asked the following voting intention question first in October and again in the past week:

- If a Canadian federal election were held today, would you vote for the candidate of the Liberal Party, the Progressive Conservative Party, the New Democratic Party or another party?

Respondents who did not express a preference were asked a follow-up question:

- Would you say that at the present time you are at least leaning or slightly favorable to one of the parties?

*Source: Globe and Mail*, 10 November 1988.

*Note:* Environics poll conducted between 3 and 8 November.

indication of the significance of the 15, 17 and 29 October dates. Fortunately, readers could refer to the short text accompanying the graph; otherwise no one would have understood a thing!

These examples illustrate some of the difficulties dailies experience in providing graphic presentations of public opinion trends. During the entire 1988 election campaign, we noted major variations among newspapers; this problem also occurred on television. If a graph is worth a thousand words, graphs presented in 1988 were far from explicit. It would therefore seem apt that graphic artists follow certain rules covering presentation of graphs in which the scales used and the dates the polls were conducted would be taken into account.

## TELEVISING POLL RESULTS

While attention to poll results on Canadian televised news and public affairs programs has undoubtedly been increasing, data are fragmentary. Jacques Gerstlé notes that in France during the 106 days of the 1988 presidential campaign, channel TF1 newscasts mentioned 70 polls: 10 references were made in January, 18 in February, 23 in March and 19 in April. In comparison, in the United States during the 1988 presidential campaign, the three major networks (CBS, NBC and ABC) referred to only 25 polls. According to Gerstlé, this would confirm the popularity of political polls in France (Gerstlé 1991). The data available suggest that the figures for Canada are similar to those for the United States during the comparable period.

The results of seven polls were aired on television during the 1988 campaign: five by Insight Canada for CTV and two by Canadian Facts for CBC/Radio-Canada. As we were unable to obtain Insight Canada's research reports, we did not review their televised presentations. We did obtain reports for the two Canadian Facts polls, however, so we were in a position to compare presentations on the French and English networks.

On Sunday, 16 October, Radio-Canada and CBC presented special one-hour programs highlighting the results of the Canadian Facts poll of 7 to 12 October 1988. There were some differences in the way the two programs were structured. First, on the English network, the results of the question on voting intentions were revealed at the beginning of the program, whereas viewers of the French network had to wait until the end of the program to find this out. Second, the poll methodology was not explicit on the English network, whereas on the French network the program hosts presented it this way:

| | |
|---|---|
| Bernard Derome: | First let's explain the methodology of this poll. It is a CBC poll conducted by a firm called Réalités canadiennes/Canadian Facts. It is a big poll! |
| Daniel Lessard: | The poll was conducted among 2 467 people through telephone interviews lasting about 20 minutes each. We contacted 900 more people than most polls do. That explains why the margin of error is very small; it is only 2 percent. This poll was conducted from Friday the 7th of October to Wednesday the 12th, and the sample of respondents, chosen randomly, is representative of the Canadian electorate. |

This was a commendable effort to present the technical aspects of the poll in accordance with CBC standards, even though these standards fall short of those prescribed by university researchers, survey experts, polling organizations, and print and electronic journalists. Nevertheless, the presentation of the methodology, which came at the beginning of the program "Décision '88," included the name of the sponsor, the name of the organization commissioned to collect the information, the number of respondents, the collection method, the duration of the interview, the margin of error, the period during which the polling took place, the sampling method and a description of the population.

Unfortunately, however, the rest of the program did not live up to the introduction. First, the wording of the questions was either left to the host to explain or avoided entirely. Both networks used only percentages in their graphic presentations of the results. None of the tables showed viewers how many people answered the questions, how many refused to answer or how many said they did not know how they were going to vote. Furthermore, there was no way of knowing whether the results obtained and the spreads in the percentages were statistically significant, given that the margin of error differed from one table to another. The difficulty was compounded when regional trends were presented: the number of people interviewed in each region remained a mystery. Finally, the question concerning voting intentions was the only one in which the proportions of undecided voters (10 percent) and refusals (4 percent) were given; there was even an effort to give the results for the Montreal region.

Another difference in the presentations of the two networks was the commentary on and interpretation of the results; again, the French network made a better choice than the English network. In French, participants at a round table hosted by the journalist Simon Durivage, commented for about six minutes after each set of results was presented. The three guests were candidates Lucien Bouchard, then of the Progressive Conservatives, Raymond Garneau of the Liberals and Phillip Edmonston of the New Democrats. The discussion was lively, and the interpretation of results was varied and spiced with a partisan flavour. Viewers knew where the round table participants stood.

The English network chose to use interviews, searching out comments on various aspects of the campaign from Canadians across the country. For example, Peterborough, Ontario, was presented to viewers as a city often used as a test market for new products. Why not get the opinion of its citizens on the election campaign! Viewers were also introduced to two polling organizations: Decima Research, pollster for the Progressive Conservatives, and Martin Goldfarb Ltd., pollster for the Liberals. The New Democratic Party's use of a U.S.-developed computer program was also shown. The use of selected commentary and documentary elements gave the program the look of a straw poll; the poll results were little more than a pretext for presenting interviews with individuals with differing points of view. What were the criteria used to select interview subjects? Does the attempt to present diverging points of view on one campaign theme, such as free trade, not tend to polarize public opinion, regardless of the actual unity or diversity of opinion on the issues? A poll is a tool for promoting public discussion; the onus is on the television networks to find program formats that permit contrasting interpretations of poll data. From this perspective, the format chosen by Radio-Canada clearly seems more appropriate than that chosen by the CBC.

The CTV network's treatment of the five Insight Canada Research polls of 14, 21 and 31 October and 11 and 19 November was relatively similar, the results having been given in almost the same format, except for the methodology. The news reader first presented the main results on voting intentions; this was followed by the position of various parties at the regional level; then came a discussion with journalist Pamela Wallin, the network's national affairs correspondent, on the results of the various survey questions. A table accompanied each set of her comments.

There are some advantages to the format chosen by CTV. First, because only one polling organization was selected, the viewer could be relatively confident that the same method was used from one survey to the next; in other words, it is easier to compare surveys conducted by the same firm than those conducted by different ones, as a polling firm generally uses similar methodology for all its surveys. Second, this approach encourages comparisons between polls; thus, during the 21 October broadcast, voting intentions were compared with the 14 October results. During this broadcast, the news reader presented the poll results and compared them with previous ones, highlighting the gains and losses for each party.

The main weakness lies in the use of regional data. During the 21 October broadcast, two headlines accompanied the news: one concerned the situation of the parties in Ontario, where the Progressive Conservatives were holding their lead with 36 percent of the support, while the Liberals and New Democrats were neck-and-neck. The other dealt with the very poor performance of the Liberals in the West, where they had only 14 percent of voter support, historically the party's weakest performance in this region. However, as no indication was given of the number of respondents in Ontario and in the West, it is difficult to know the real margin of error.

In addition, the methodology was presented in summary form on each broadcast, with no consistent format being followed. Four examples illustrate this observation. During the 21 October broadcast, the opening remarks by Lloyd Robertson were on the Insight Canada Research poll conducted between 13 and 20 October:

> A national election poll shows the NDP moving to second place with the Liberals dropping to third. That's the main difference from last week in this continuing survey commissioned by CTV and conducted by Insight Canada Research. The sample was taken over the last seven days.

The methodological information given on this poll was relatively limited.

All one learns is that CTV was the sponsor and that Insight Canada Research conducted the survey. The period of the interviews was not stated clearly; viewers may have been tempted to conclude that the final interview occurred on 21 October, given that this date appeared on the comparative table of voting intentions. All other methodological items that we mentioned earlier were also absent.

The 26 October broadcast of the results of a poll conducted between 25 and 26 October, immediately following the leaders debate, presented the results on the leaders' performance and indicated that the margin of error for this survey was 4.1 percent. The 30 October broadcast of the results of the 27 and 30 October Insight poll revealed that there were 1 100 respondents and that the survey had been conducted over the past four days. In this case, ambiguity concerning the date of the final interview added an element of confusion.

Finally, for the last Insight Canada Research poll of the campaign, broadcast on 19 November, two days before the election, the announcer presented a slightly more explicit description of the methodology, emphasizing that "The survey was done between Wednesday and today. Insight Canada polls 2 700 eligible voters. It says the results are accurate between plus or minus 3 percent, 19 times out of 20." This time, it was specified that the survey was conducted between 16 and 19 November, which included the day of the broadcast. The number of respondents and margin of error were identified.

The same difficulties with the CBC presentation of the Canadian Facts polls were apparent in CTV's presentation of the Insight polls. Perhaps most disturbing is that, unlike CBC's polling information, which was available to anyone interested and persistent enough to track it down, information produced for a private television broadcaster can be withheld, even if the results were the subject of public broadcasts. In this connection, the broadcasters, in collaboration with polling organizations, could take the initiative by freely circulating this information among the public.

Irving Crespi, who was a special adviser to the NBC network and worked for Gallup for nearly 20 years, suggests that for some U.S. programs, such as "Meet the Press," "Face the Nation" and the "MacNeil-Lehrer News Hour," it would even be possible to include an audience. Crespi says guests should be given a copy of poll results before the program, and the emphasis during interviews should be on analysing the data and exchanging ideas on their significance. Furthermore, the public could be invited to request copies of polling reports. Crespi offered these suggestions to make televised poll results more dynamic and interesting (Mendelsohn and Crespi 1970; Crespi

1989, 129). The use of explanatory captions at the bottom of the television screen, such as those used during the last presidential election in France, would be another way of presenting methodological information on polls.

## CONCLUSION

A review of Canadian daily newspapers reveals significant shortcomings in the journalistic treatment of polls. The methodological information provided is too sketchy (if it is present at all) to allow the public to assess the quality and reliability of the results presented. It is surprising to find, 10 years after the Canadian Daily Newspaper Publishers Association adopted a code of practice for dealing with polls, that few of the dailies we reviewed follow the code completely. The failure to provide information as basic as the size of the initial sample, the rejection rate, the response rate and the weighting variables used is simply unacceptable. Only one daily, the *Globe and Mail*, rises above the others, partly because of its use of a methodological box and partly, no doubt, because the researchers who conduct the polls are also involved in presenting the results. These efforts still fell short of the ideal, however, which leaves us wondering how media treatment of polls can improve, even if the task is entrusted to journalists with extensive experience in analysing polling results.

Newspaper headlines generally reflect poll results accurately, usually emphasizing voting intentions, but graphic presentations are clearly less than adequate. In our view, the polling organizations should be responsible for the graphic presentation of their findings. Even so, the print media could make a start by ensuring that their graphics are prepared by competent people. The same applies to television, which leans toward simplification to the extent that viewers have trouble getting the full story even with the help of commentators. Radio reports are undoubtedly even more difficult to follow.

# 8

## REGIONAL, PROVINCIAL, LOCAL, CONSTITUENCY, THEMATIC AND PARTISAN POLLS
### The Campaign's Forgotten Polls

National polls are not the only polls reported in the media; there are also regional, provincial, local, marginal (taken in selected key ridings), constituency and exit polls, as well as straw polls. To this list we should add thematic polls on specific issues (free trade or the leaders debates) and partisan polls conducted by polling organizations associated with the political parties (e.g., Goldfarb for the Liberals and Decima Research for the Progressive Conservatives); the latter polls tend to be released to the media largely for strategic, partisan reasons.

Three types of polls in particular have multiplied in recent years: exit polls, marginal polls in the ridings most likely to change party allegiance and polls conducted in specific constituencies. The British example is a good indicator of the volume of these polls.

The 1987 election campaign in Britain saw the largest exit poll ever conducted; it was carried out by Harris/ITN. The poll surveyed 4 500 respondents in some 50 constituencies (Waller 1987). More recently, exit polls in Poland predicted Lech Walesa's victory. In the polls conducted in marginal ridings, the sampling base is the population of a certain riding considered a barometer of the election outcome. However, this phenomenon is relatively new in England, occurring mainly in the last two elections, those of 1984 and 1987.

In 1984, Harris conducted 40 constituency polls for the periodical *Weekend World;* although the number declined to 20 in 1987, these polls received much more media attention than in 1984. As Pippa Norris (1989) points out, polls conducted during earlier elections were generally badly presented by the media, often giving the impression that they were based on national samples. These polls received greater attention in 1987, apparently because of the belief that strategic voting behaviour makes certain ridings more important than others in determining election results. This hypothesis also suggests that it is pointless to attempt to predict the number of seats using conventional methods because the electoral dynamic changes according to the likelihood of change in marginal seats.

The constituency poll also attempts to identify the "hot" ridings and to predict which party has the best chance of winning them. These polls are the subject of much criticism, however, particularly in relation to methodology. The major difficulty is determining the characteristics of hotly contested seats. The factor used most often to define marginal ridings is the spread in the number of votes or in the percentage of the vote that separated the two principal political parties at the last election in the constituency. Several criteria can be used to select these ridings: the majority obtained by the main parties in the last election, ridings in which the contest is between only two candidates, ridings won by the governing party in the last election, and the ridings in which the incumbents are running again.

During the 1987 British election, Gallup conducted four polls in which the sampling base was the 72 ridings where the Conservatives had won the narrowest majorities (less than 10 percent) in the 1984 contest. The other British polling organizations instead chose the ridings in which the Conservatives had obtained the largest majorities – as much as 16 percent (NOP), 20 percent (Harris and MORI) and 24 percent (*Newsnight*). Thus, MORI selected 73 ridings, *Newsnight* 60 and NOP 52; only Harris used different sampling bases in the four polls of marginal seats that it conducted (polls in 100, 68, 67 and 66 ridings). It is, therefore, impossible to compare all the polls conducted and even more difficult to establish the sampling bases, as this requires a knowledge of population characteristics in every riding polled.

Polls in specific constituencies also attracted greater interest during the last British elections. About 78 polls of this type were conducted in 52 different ridings by about 15 organizations (Waller 1989, 239). The attraction of this type of poll is often that it can assist the search for a barometer riding whose population is fairly similar to that of a whole region, province or country. Seventeen of these polls correctly predicted the winning party within a margin of error of 3 percent; another 13 missed the mark entirely.

The growth of this type of poll in Great Britain suggests that it may not be long before Canada follows the trend; in the 1988 federal election campaign, the strategy of the Liberal Party of Canada was to focus on hot ridings, although the experience was inconclusive, mostly because the party wanted to save money (Hoy 1989, 63–64). During the same election, at least 37 "other" polls were published in the daily or weekly press. These polls, along with the methodological information published with each, are listed in table 1.13. As shown in table 1.14, the sampling base of these polls, in order of frequency, was as follows: a metropolitan area, nine polls; a province, eight; a group of constituencies, six; one riding, three; Canada-wide (thematic polls), three; one target population, four; one region, two. In two cases, the sampling base was not clearly indicated.

To our knowledge, no exit poll was made public and no poll was conducted on a sample of marginal ridings. We were able to find only two constituency polls.

Our analysis has largely ignored the comments of participants in partisan politics on the subject of certain polls, in particular, published or broadcast comments by party leaders, candidates, political organizers and party supporters maintaining that according to their polls, one party or candidate is in the lead, closing in on the leaders, or running neck-and-neck with the opponent. On more than one occasion parties have used this stratagem of arguing that their polls differ from the latest polls made public, to reduce the impact of unfavourable national polls. This is obviously only one of many tactics used by all parties to discredit the adversary and to influence electors during a campaign. In this sense, polls are often the object of heated discussion, another factor that can call their validity and accuracy into question.

In summary, a large number of polls other than national ones were unveiled in the media over the course of the 1988 election. Our list is certainly not exhaustive, although we have attempted to include as many polls as possible. Our data come from the files of the Library of Parliament press clipping service in Ottawa. Our primary objective is to look more closely at who is involved in the polling scene and to clarify the characteristics and importance of these numerous other polls. Among the other polls that were made public, we must ask whether all were genuine polls that followed tested sampling methods, then evaluate how they were presented by the media and assess, as in the case of Canada-wide polls, the accuracy of their predictions.

**Table 1.13**
**Other polls published during the 1988 federal election**

| | Sponsor | Collection method | Population sample | Ineligible people | Rejection rate | Respondents | Response rate | Margin of error | Weighting variables | Sampling method |
|---|---|---|---|---|---|---|---|---|---|---|
| 1. Segma-Lavalin 2–4 October | Super Hebdo | Telephone | Metropolitan Montreal | n.a. | n.a. | 428 | n.a. | 2–5 | Language, sex | n.a. |
| 2. Gallup Inc. 6–8 October | Toronto Star | Telephone | Metropolitan Toronto | n.a. | n.a. | 1 017 | n.a. | 4.0 | n.a. | n.a. |
| 3. IQOP 10–12 October | CHRC (Québec) | Telephone | Charlesbourg Louis-Hébert Montmorency-Orléans Lévis Québec-Est Langelier | n.a. | n.a. | 500 | n.a. | n.a. | n.a. | |
| 4. Segma-Lavalin 13–17 October | Super Hebdo | Telephone | Metropolitan Montreal | n.a. | n.a. | 431 | 62 | 2–5 | Language | Random |
| 5. CROP 13–17 October | La Presse TVA | Telephone | Que. | n.a. | n.a. | 1 006 | n.a. | 3.0 | n.a. | n.a. |
| 6. Sorécom 14–22 October | Le Soleil | Telephone | Que. (1 724) | 232 | n.a. | 1 015 | 68 | 1.38–3.16 | Region, age, sex | Random |
| 7. Jean Jolicoeur 8 weeks–summer | n.a. | Telephone | Que. | n.a. | n.a. | 2 840 | n.a. | n.a. | Region, language | Proportional |

**Table 1.13** (cont'd)
**Other polls published during the 1988 federal election**

| | Sponsor | Collection method | Population sample | Ineligible people | Rejection rate | Respondents | Response rate | Margin of error | Weighting variables | Sampling method |
|---|---|---|---|---|---|---|---|---|---|---|
| 8. Norman Ruff 22–23 October | U. of Victoria | n.a. | Victoria Saanich | n.a. | n.a. | 187 | n.a. | n.a. | n.a. | Straw poll |
| 9. Factor Research Group Inc. Post-debate | None | n.a. | Ottawa–Carleton Outaouais | n.a. | n.a. | 403 | n.a. | 4.0 | n.a. | n.a. |
| 10. Omnifacts Research Ltd. October | Halifax *Chronicle-Herald* ATV | n.a. | NS, NB, PEI (1 219) | n.a. | n.a. | 860 | n.a. | n.a. | n.a. | n.a. |
| 11. Insight Canada Research 25–26 October | CTV | Telephone | Canada | n.a. | n.a. | n.a. | n.a. | 4.1 | n.a. | n.a. |
| 12. Gallup Inc. 26–29 Octobe | Subscribers | In person | Canada | n.a. | n.a. | 1 026 | n.a. | 4.0 | n.a. | n.a. |
| 13. Prairie Research Associates Inc. 31 Oct.–4 Nov. | n.a. | Telephone | Man. | n.a. | n.a. | 805 | n.a. | 3.5 | n.a. | n.a. |
| 14. Marktrend Marketing Research Inc ?–3 November | n.a. | Telephone | BC | n.a. | n.a. | 507 | n.a. | 4.5 | Region | n.a. |

Table 1.13 (cont'd)
**Other polls published during the 1988 federal election**

| | Sponsor | Collection method | Population sample | Ineligible people | Rejection rate | Respondents | Response rate | Margin of error | Weighting variables | Sampling method |
|---|---|---|---|---|---|---|---|---|---|---|
| 15. CROP 1–6 November | *La Presse* Télé-Métropole | Telephone | Outremont Ahuntsic Chambly Rosemont Laurier–Sainte-Marie | n.a. | n.a. | 1 599 | 76 | 6.0 | Sex, age | Random |
| 16. SOM 1–7 November | *This Week in Business* | Telephone | Que. | n.a. | n.a. | 1 031 | n.a. | 3.3 | n.a. | n.a. |
| 17. McKay Goettler and Associates 2–6 November | CJWW (Saskatoon) | n.a. | Saskatoon– Clark's Crossing Saskatoon–Dundum Saskatoon–Humboldt | n.a. | n.a. | 646 | n.a. | 10.0/5.0 | n.a. | n.a. |
| 18. Martin Goldfarb 4–7 November | Penta Stolp Corp. | n.a. | Metropolitan Toronto | n.a. | n.a. | 800 | n.a. | n.a. | n.a. | n.a. |
| 19. IQOP 4–8 November | *Le Soleil* | Telephone | Ridings: Quebec (6) Central (3) South shore (2) North shore (2) St. Lawrence Lowlands & Gaspé (5) Côte-Nord (4 479) | n.a. | n.a. | 2 040 | 46 | 2.2 | Voters by sub-regions | n.a. |

**Table 1.13 (cont'd)**
**Other polls published during the 1988 federal election**

| | Sponsor | Collection method | Population sample | Ineligible people | Rejection rate | Respondents | Response rate | Margin of error | Weighting variables | Sampling method |
|---|---|---|---|---|---|---|---|---|---|---|
| 20. Sorécom 4–13 November | Le Soleil | Telephone | Que. (2 064) | 303 | n.a. | 1 170 | 66 | 1.23–2.82 | Region | Random |
| 21. Sorécom 6–10 November | Montreal Daily News | Telephone | Ridings: Montreal (32) | n.a. | n.a. | 827 | n.a. | 1.5–3.5 | Sub-region | n.a. |
| 22. Criterion Research Corp. 7–9 November | Edmonton Journal | n.a. | Edmonton–Strathcona Southwest Northwest North East Southeast | n.a. | n.a. | 862 | n.a. | 3.3 | Voters, riding, age, sex | n.a. |
| 23. Environics 9–13 November | Brockville Recorder and Times | n.a. | Leeds–Grenville | n.a. | n.a. | 406 | n.a. | 4.8 | n.a. | n.a. |
| 24. Université du Québec à Hull P. Aubry and R. Laurendeau 11–13 November | Le Droit | n.a. | Hull–Aylmer Gatineau–La Lièvre | n.a. | n.a. | 498 | n.a. | 3.0 | French-speaking | n.a. |
| 25. CROP 11–14 November | La Presse | Telephone | Que. | n.a. | n.a. | 1 051 | 72 | 3.0 | Region, sex, language | Random |

Table 1.13 (cont'd)
Other polls published during the 1988 federal election

| | Sponsor | Collection method | Population sample | Ineligible people | Rejection rate | Respondents | Response rate | Margin of error | Weighting variables | Sampling method |
|---|---|---|---|---|---|---|---|---|---|---|
| 26. Sask Research Associates 13–16 November | CK Radio | Telephone | Regina–Wascana Regina–Qu'Appelle Regina–Lumsden | n.a. | n.a. | 275 168 162 | n.a. | 4.0 6.0 6.0 | n.a. | n.a. |
| 27. Optima Research 2 weeks | n.a. | n.a. | Ridings: Outaouais (3) Ottawa–Carleton (8) | n.a. | n.a. | 1 713 | n.a. | 3.0 | n.a. | n.a. |
| 28. Factor Research Group Inc. 14–15 November | n.a. | Telephone | n.a. | n.a. | n.a. | 404 | n.a. | 4.0 | n.a. | n.a. |
| 29. IQOP 15–16 November | CHRC | Telephone | Quebec area (1 000) | 259 | n.a. | 504 | 59 | 4.4 | n.a. | n.a. |
| 30. Québec-Est Liberal Association November | Rémi Bujold, Liberal candidate | Telephone | Québec-Est | n.a. | n.a. | 326 | n.a. | n.a. | n.a. | n.a. |
| 31. Canadian Peace Pledge Campaign Start of campaign | None | Postal | Candidates in 180 ridings | n.a. | n.a. | 146 (61 NDP, 45 Lib., 40 PC) | n.a. | n.a. | n.a. | n.a. |

**Table 1.13** (cont'd)
**Other polls published during the 1988 federal election**

| | Sponsor | Collection method | Population sample | Ineligible people | Rejection rate | Respondents | Response rate | Margin of error | Weighting variables | Sampling method |
|---|---|---|---|---|---|---|---|---|---|---|
| 32. Segma-Lavalin 12–16 November | *Journal de Montréal* | Telephone | Metropolitan Montréal (1 778) | 807 | n.a. | 484 | 50 | 4.5 | Sex, age | Proba-bilities |
| 33. Compas Inc. 6 weeks–summer | n.a. | In person | The "élite" | n.a. | n.a. | 404 | n.a. | n.a. | n.a. | n.a. |
| 34. Toronto's Better Business Bureau Recent poll | None | n.a. | Brokers, wholesalers, retailers, manufacturers, construction contractors | n.a. | n.a. | 250 | n.a. | n.a. | n.a. | n.a. |
| 35. *Winnipeg Free Press* October–November | None | In person | Voters | n.a. | n.a. | 100 | n.a. | n.a. | n.a. | Straw poll |
| 36. Decima Research October | *Financial Times* | Telephone | Canada | n.a. | n.a. | 1 100 | n.a. | n.a. | n.a. | n.a. |
| 37. Martin Goldfarb not available | Baton Broadcasting | Telephone | n.a. | n.a. | n.a. | n.a. | n.a. | 4.0 | n.a. | n.a. |

*Note:* n.a. = not available.

Table 1.14
**Sampling base for regional, provincial, constituency and partisan polls**

| Sampling base | Description | Number of polls |
|---|---|---|
| Constituency | Leeds–Grenville | 1 |
| | Québec-Est | 1 |
| | Victoria/Saanich[a] | 1 |
| Metropolitan area | Montreal | 4 |
| | Toronto | 2 |
| | Quebec | 2 |
| | *Winnipeg Free Press*[a] | 1 |
| Region | Atlantic provinces | 1 |
| | Hull–Aylmer/Gatineau–La Lièvre | 1 |
| Province | Quebec | 6 |
| | British Columbia | 1 |
| | Manitoba | 1 |
| Constituency groups | 5 Montreal ridings | 1 |
| | 3 Saskatoon ridings | 1 |
| | 3 Regina ridings | 1 |
| | 6 Edmonton ridings | 1 |
| | 19 Quebec peripheral ridings | 1 |
| | 11 Ottawa–Carleton and Outaouais ridings | 1 |
| Whole of Canada | Thematic polls | 3 |
| Target population | Candidates from 180 ridings | 1 |
| | Toronto decision makers | 1 |
| | Small and medium-sized businesses in Toronto area | 1 |
| Undefined | Factor Research Group Inc. | 1 |
| | Martin Goldfarb | 1 |
| Total | | 36 |

[a]Straw poll.

## PRESENTING "OTHER" POLLS

We applied the assessment grid proposed by the polling committee of the Regroupement québécois des sciences sociales to the "other" polls to see whether their journalistic treatment differs from that of the national polls. Given that other polls receive less attention from the media – coverage is limited in the sense that fewer lines are written about them and they are given less prominence than national stories – we might expect, for example, less attention paid to methodological standards. Moreover, standards may not be as rigorous because many of these polls are conducted by regionally based polling organizations with less media experience.

## Sponsors and Interview Dates

The regional distribution of "other" polls published during the 1988 campaign is shown in table 1.15.

The preponderance of Quebec polls is perhaps explained by the large number of polling firms in the province (including CROP, Sorécom, IQOP, SOM, Jean Jolicoeur et associés, and Segma-Lavalin). Furthermore, the Ontario-based polling organizations generally conduct most of the national polls, leaving little room in that market for other organizations. In the 1984 election, organizations like CROP, Sorécom and the Centre for Polling at the Carleton University School of Journalism conducted 6 of the 12 national polls; in 1988, Angus Reid conducted 4, and all the others were carried out by Toronto-based firms. The change is striking enough to raise the question of whether we are witnessing the concentration of national polling in central Canada.[11]

Table 1.16 shows seven instances of "other" polls for which the name of the sponsor was not clearly identified and four for which there was no sponsor. In other cases, polling firms revealed survey results to the media to gain publicity (Factor Research), to attract public sympathy to a cause (Toronto Better Business Bureau, Canadian Peace Pledge Campaign) or simply to make news (*Winnipeg Free Press*). The print media were the principal clients for these polls. Unlike Canada-wide polls, few of these "other" polls (13 percent of cases) were sponsored by radio and television networks. Their sponsors included political parties, private business and an economic development organization.

We were not surprised to find the highest number of provincial polls (43 percent) in Quebec; several Quebec polling firms have existed for years and are just as active in federal and provincial elections as in municipal elections. But it was surprising to see how few polling organizations outside Quebec have conducted regional or provincial polls and that even a firm such as Angus Reid, whose offices are in Winnipeg, limited itself to national polls (although it did do an over-sample of British Columbia in its first national poll of the campaign to gain a better picture of voter behaviour in that province).

While most of the poll stories examined did report the dates of the survey interviews, a significant number did not, as the following figures indicate:

| | | |
|---|---|---|
| Clearly identified | 25 | (68%) |
| Unclear | 9 | (24%) |
| Not indicated | 3 | ( 8%) |
| Total | 37 | (100%) |

In one case in three, therefore, interview dates were reported incorrectly in the media. Comparing Sorécom's polling reports with coverage

Table 1.15
Regional distribution of "other" polls published during
the 1988 federal election campaign

| Province/region | Number of polls |
|---|---|
| Quebec | 16 |
| Ontario | 6 |
| Prairies | 5 |
| British Columbia | 2 |
| Atlantic | 1 |
| Canada | 4 |
| Not indicated | 3 |
| Total | 37 |

Table 1.16
Principal sponsors

| | Number of polls | | | | | | | Total | |
|---|---|---|---|---|---|---|---|---|---|
| | Print media | Tele- vision | Print media and television | Radio | None | Other | n.a. | N | % |
| Quebec | 11 | 0 | 2 | 2 | 0 | 1 | 0 | 16 | 43 |
| Ontario | 2 | 0 | 0 | 0 | 1 | 2 | 1 | 6 | 16 |
| Prairies | 2 | 0 | 0 | 1 | 0 | 0 | 2 | 5 | 14 |
| British Columbia | 0 | 0 | 0 | 0 | 0 | 1 | 1 | 2 | 5 |
| Atlantic provinces | 0 | 0 | 1 | 0 | 0 | 0 | 0 | 1 | 3 |
| Canada | 1 | 1 | 0 | 0 | 1 | 0 | 1 | 4 | 11 |
| Undetermined | 0 | 1 | 0 | 0 | 0 | 0 | 2 | 3 | 8 |
| Total *N* | 16 | 2 | 3 | 3 | 2 | 4 | 7 | 37 | |
| % | 43 | 5 | 8 | 8 | 5 | 11 | 19 | | 100 |

*Note:* n.a. = not available.

by the dailies *Le Soleil*, the Montreal *Gazette* and the *Montreal Daily News*,
we note that none of the newspapers gave the correct dates in their
articles. In the first case, headlines on 18 November 1988 in *Le Soleil*
and the *Gazette* indicated the Sorécom poll was conducted from 4 to 14
November (Forgues 1988; *Gazette* 1988); the Sorécom report shows the
dates as 4 to 13 November. In the second case, the *Daily News* of 14

November indicated the poll was conducted between 6 and 8 November, whereas the Sorécom report says 6 to 10 November (*Montreal Daily News* 1988, 3). Because interview dates are one of the important elements enabling analysts to follow the evolution of voting intentions during a campaign, concerns about whether this problem is widespread are not unfounded. The validity of certain polls can also be questioned when interviews extend over several weeks or even months (Jean Jolicoeur et associés, eight weeks; Compas Inc., six weeks; Optima Research, two weeks; *Winnipeg Free Press*, two months).

### Collection Method, Population Studied, Sample Size, Number of Ineligible Respondents, Rejection Rate and Sampling Method

The collection method was given in only 27 polls (73 percent). Twenty-three polls were conducted by telephone, three through face-to-face interviews, and only one by mail-in questionnaire. This information was reported by all the newspapers that carried the results of polls conducted by Quebec firms. The 10 polls for which this information was missing were published in the *Globe and Mail* (two), the *Ottawa Citizen* (two), the Victoria *Times Colonist*, the Halifax *Chronicle-Herald*, the Saskatoon *Star Phoenix*, the *Edmonton Journal*, *Le Droit* and the *Toronto Sun*. In short, this basic information, which was included in published reports on all the national polls, received less attention from newspapers.

In 25 cases, a description of the population studied was given; this information was absent for only two polls, one by Factor Research, published in the *Ottawa Citizen*, and the other by Goldfarb, published in *Le Droit*. In many instances, however, the description was inadequate. For example, when a poll is conducted in a metropolitan area like Toronto or Montreal, population definitions must be clear, particularly since they are bound to vary from one poll to another.

The mail-in poll of the campaign was conducted by the Canadian Peace Pledge Campaign; the results were published in the *Globe and Mail*. Readers were not told, however, whether a questionnaire was sent to all candidates in the 180 ridings selected. The same applies to the poll by the Toronto Better Business Bureau. We know that the poll surveyed brokers, wholesalers, retailers, manufacturers and construction contractors of Toronto, but we do not know the importance of each of these groups in that city. The Compas poll, for example, states that their sample was composed of 234 public servants, 101 councillors, 41 academics and 28 journalists ($N = 404$). But is this a representative sample of Canadian élites? On the whole, this aspect of methodology requires more careful attention by journalists and polling organizations, because imprecision at this level makes interpretation of results extremely hazardous.

In only six cases was information on the size of the sample published along with poll results. Five of the polls were conducted by Quebec organizations (Sorécom, two; IQOP, two; Segma-Lavalin, one), and one used a sample from the Atlantic provinces (Omnifacts Research). However, only four reports on these polls also included the number of ineligible people contacted: two Sorécom polls, one IQOP poll and one Segma-Lavalin poll. No published results of any poll included the rejection rate. Although these figures are low, they are better than the performance on national polls: in no instance did we find the size of the sample and the number of ineligible people.

Finally, with respect to sampling methods, here, too, the tendency was toward more descriptive reporting than in the case of national polls. Again, it was the Quebec press that was more attentive to the need to provide this information. This information was reported for nine polls (24 percent of cases); of these, seven were polls conducted by Quebec polling institutes (CROP, two; Segma-Lavalin, two; Sorécom, two; Jean Jolicoeur, one). The two remaining polls were conducted by the University of Victoria and the *Winnipeg Free Press*. The first was a poll by political scientist Norman Ruff that was clearly identified as a straw poll but in which readers were not cautioned about explicit difficulties in interpreting the results of such surveys. The second involved interviews by the *Winnipeg Free Press* with 100 of its readers in the Manitoba capital; here again, even though the main elements of the survey were described, readers should have been informed more fully about the limitations of such surveys.

### Number of Respondents, Response Rate, Margin of Error and Data Adjustment

Except for one poll each by Martin Goldfarb, Insight Canada Research and the Toronto Better Business Bureau, all published reports on "other" polls included the number of respondents. In several instances the size of the sample, at around 500 respondents or even fewer, seems relatively small, particularly the polls conducted by IQOP (500 and 504 respondents), Marktrend Marketing (507), Université du Québec à Hull (498), Segma-Lavalin (428, 431 and 484), Factor Research (403 and 404), Environics (406), Compas (404) and the Liberal Party of Canada (326). The Canada Peace Pledge Campaign mail survey had only 146 respondents, and the straw polls by the University of Victoria and the *Winnipeg Free Press* had only 187 and 100 respondents, respectively. Overall, 15 of the polls or surveys had fewer than 507 respondents, two had between 508 and 800 respondents (McKay Goettler and Sask Research).

Unlike the national polls, none of which had fewer than 800 respondents (except for the second stage of the Environics panel), half the regional polls had numbers of respondents below generally accepted standards. This does not mean that the quality of these polls is necessarily inferior, but it does mean that their interpretation and reporting require closer attention.

Only eight polls, all conducted by Quebec organizations, reported their response rates. Margins of error should also be given and calculated with precision; this information was not available in 11 polls. Moreover, the margin of error is a function of not only the number of respondents but also the sampling method. For example, in a poll conducted in five Montreal constituencies, where the number of respondents varied between 303 and 344 for each riding, CROP correctly calculated the real margin of error based on a sample composed of electors from different regions. If this poll had a total of 1 599 respondents, its margin of error remained around 6 percent.

The results of the Sask Research poll of three Regina constituencies, as presented in the Regina *Leader-Post,* also indicated the margin of error for each riding. The report on the McKay Goettler poll did likewise, but its presentation in the Saskatoon *Star Phoenix* was contradictory, to say the least. One article read, "This poll is considered accurate 19 out of 20 times, with an error margin of five per cent" (Greenshields 1988b). But an article on the front page of the same newspaper said that the poll "is considered accurate nine times out of 10 with an error margin of 10 per cent" (Greenshields 1988a). As the two articles were written by the same journalist, the least that can be said is that confusion reigned!

Finally, we noted only 13 of the polls were accompanied in the press by information on data adjustment and weighting factors. Eleven of these polls were conducted by Quebec organizations, the other two by Marktrend Marketing Research and Criterion Research.

## POLLING ACCURACY

One of the persistent questions on the topic of regional and local polls concerns the degree of their precision. Were these polls successful in predicting voting intentions within the prescribed margins of error? Six polls at the provincial level dealt with voting intentions: four in Quebec, one in Manitoba and one in British Columbia. The four Quebec polls, two by CROP and two by Sorécom, predicted a Progressive Conservative victory with an average of 45.8 percent of the vote; Liberal support stood at 30 percent; that of the NDP, at 22.5 percent. In Manitoba, the Prairie Research poll predicted that 25.2 percent of the vote would go to the Liberals, 21 percent to the Progressive Conservatives and 17.5

percent to the New Democrats. In British Columbia, the Marktrend Marketing poll considered it a tight race between the Progressive Conservatives and the New Democrats, running neck-and-neck at 34 percent, followed by the Liberals at 28 percent.

In Quebec, the Progressive Conservative share of the vote (53 percent) was underestimated by 7.2 percent, Liberal support was predicted correctly (30 percent), and the New Democratic vote, at 14 percent, was overestimated by 8.5 percent. In Manitoba, the Progressive Conservative party obtained 37 percent of the vote; the Liberal party, 36 percent; and the NDP, 21 percent. Once again, the Progressive Conservative vote was underestimated, as was support for the Liberals. Finally, in British Columbia, the NDP obtained 37 percent of the vote, followed by the Progressive Conservatives at 34 percent and the Liberals at 21 percent; the race was as tight as predicted (for detailed results of the election, see Clarke et al. 1991, 158). On the whole, the discrepancies between predictions and actual voter support were decidedly outside the margins of error for each of the categories. Therefore, future polls of this nature must be interpreted with caution.

In metropolitan Toronto, for example, the only poll of a sample drawn from the population of this area was conducted by Gallup at the beginning of the campaign, between 6 and 8 October. The poll gave 41 percent of the vote to the Progressive Conservatives, 32 percent to the Liberals and 26 percent to the NDP. In fact, the election results were as follows: Liberals 41.9 percent of the vote and 12 seats; Progressive Conservatives, 36.9 percent of the vote and nine seats; and the NDP, 18.9 percent of the vote and two seats.

On the island of Montreal, the Progressive Conservatives obtained 43.5 percent of the vote and 14 seats; the Liberals, 38.5 percent and nine seats; and the New Democrats, 13.6 percent of the vote and no seats. The first poll of the election campaign, conducted by Segma-Lavalin in the greater Montreal area, placed the Progressive Conservatives ahead, with 30 percent of the vote, followed by the Liberals and the NDP with 22 percent each (before redistribution of undecided respondents). The Sorécom poll, conducted from 6 to 10 November, gave the Liberals 44.5 percent of the vote and 16–19 seats on the island of Montreal; the Progressive Conservatives, 32 percent of the vote and a maximum of three seats; and the New Democrats, 19.5 percent of the vote with perhaps one seat (Duff 1988). Finally, *Le Journal de Montréal* sponsored a poll by Segma-Lavalin that gave the Progressive Conservatives 36 percent of the vote; the Liberals, 30 percent; and the NDP, 15 percent. This last poll produced a reasonably accurate forecast, but the predictions of the other two were completely erroneous.

In the Quebec City region, a poll conducted by IQOP between 10 and 12 October predicted that in the six local electoral districts (Charlesbourg, Louis-Hébert, Beauport–Montmorency–Orléans, Lévis, Québec-Est and Langelier), the Progressive Conservatives would obtain 51 percent of the vote; the NDP, 32 percent; and the Liberals, 17 percent. The results were different there as well. On 21 November, the Progressive Conservatives obtained 56.6 percent of the vote and walked away with all six seats, while the Liberals followed with 25.3 percent and the NDP with 15.9 percent. The results might suggest that the figures for the Liberal and NDP votes were transposed in error at the time the poll results were made public! The second IQOP poll was more accurate, however, predicting 46.4 percent for the Progressive Conservatives, 31.7 percent for the Liberals and 21.8 percent for the NDP; even so, the Progressive Conservative vote was still underestimated. The last IQOP poll did predict the blue sweep of the Quebec City region, however, giving 57 percent of the vote to the Progressive Conservatives, 22 percent to the Liberals and 21 percent to the NDP (L. Lemieux 1988; *Le Devoir* 1988).

CROP polled five ridings in the Montreal area between 1 and 6 November: Outremont, Ahuntsic, Rosemont, Laurier–Sainte-Marie and Chambly. CROP predicted Liberal victories in the first four ridings and a close race among the three candidates in Chambly, with the Progressive Conservatives slightly ahead of the NDP candidate, Phillip Edmonston. On election night, the results proved very different: instead of receiving 40 percent of the vote, Liberal Lucie Pépin received 34.6 percent. She was defeated by her Progressive Conservative opponent, Jean-Pierre Hogue, who received 38.6 percent instead of the predicted 25 percent. In Ahuntsic, Raymond Garneau lost by only 522 votes to Progressive Conservative candidate Nicole Roy-Arcelin; the comfortable lead of 50 percent versus 26 percent evaporated. In Rosemont, Liberal candidate Jacques Guilbault was beaten by Progressive Conservative Benoît Tremblay, although CROP had placed Tremblay in third place. In Laurier–Sainte-Marie, the Liberal candidate won the election with 37.8 percent of the vote, well below the projected 50 percent. Finally, the Progressive Conservative candidate in Chambly, Richard Grisé, won with 46.8 percent of the vote, far more than the estimated 35 percent. In all, the Progressive Conservatives won four of the five seats.

In the poll conducted between 2 and 6 November in Saskatoon, McKay Goettler predicted New Democratic wins in Saskatoon–Dundurn and Saskatoon–Humboldt and a close race between the Progressive Conservatives and the Liberals in Saskatoon–Clark's Crossing. For the three ridings, the results were predicted to be NDP, 42 percent; Progressive Conservatives, 35.1 percent; and Liberals, 22.9 percent. The New Democrats won all three constituencies, however, including Saskatoon–Clark's Crossing, where the poll had placed them behind by 15.2 percent of the vote. The general results of the election did, however, correspond quite closely to the results of the poll: NDP, 46.0 percent; Progressive Conservatives, 34.7 percent; and Liberals, 18.7 percent.

According to the Criterion Research poll conducted in Edmonton, the Progressive Conservatives should have won at least five of the six seats in the region. The poll predicted that they would obtain 30 percent of the vote across the Edmonton ridings, followed by the Liberals at 18 percent and the New Democrats at 17 percent, before redistribution of undecided respondents. In fact, the Progressive Conservatives did win five of the six ridings; the NDP won the sixth. The distribution of the vote, however, was a little different: the Progressive Conservatives obtained 42.3 percent of the vote, but the New Democratic Party finished a strong second with 26.6 percent, and the Liberals followed with 18.8 percent. The Reform Party, which had been predicted to receive a maximum of 5 percent of the vote, in fact obtained 10.7 percent.

In Regina, the Sask Research poll conducted between 13 and 16 November, one week before the election, predicted New Democratic victories in Regina–Qu'Appelle and Regina–Lumsden and a tight race in Regina–Wascana, with the New Democratic Party receiving an average in the three ridings of 44.2 percent of the vote; the Progressive Conservatives, 32.7 percent; and the Liberals, 21.9 percent. In fact, following the vote on 21 November, the NDP won two seats as predicted and obtained an average of 46.9 percent of the vote; the Progressive Conservatives won the remaining seat and 30.9 percent, while the Liberals received only 21.9 percent. Taking sample size and margin of error into account, the poll predictions were very accurate.

The Environics poll in the Ontario riding of Leeds–Grenville showed a tight race between Progressive Conservative Jennifer Cossitt, with 41 percent of the vote, and Liberal Jim Jordan, with 39 percent. The New Democratic Party vote was predicted to be only 14 percent. On the evening of the election, the tables were turned: Jim Jordan won with 43.4 percent of the vote, compared with 39 percent for the Progressive Conservative candidate. The NDP received 11.1 percent of the votes cast.

A Liberal Party of Canada poll in the riding of Québec-Est predicted that their candidate, Rémi Bujold, would win with 41 percent of the vote, followed by the Progressive Conservatives at 38 percent and the New Democrats at 21 percent. The election results were quite different. The Progressive Conservative candidate, Marcel R. Tremblay, received 55.8 percent of the vote, followed by the Liberal candidate with

25.9 percent and the NDP candidate, Jeanne Lalanne, with 14.3 percent.

Finally, a straw poll held under the auspices of political scientist Norman Ruff of the University of Victoria showed 49 percent confirmed support for the NDP, 29 percent for the Progressive Conservatives and 8 percent for the Liberals in the ridings of Victoria and Saanich–Gulf Islands. The two seats actually went to the Progressive Conservatives, but the voting pattern was different: NDP, 35.1 percent; Progressive Conservatives, 32.7 percent; and Liberals, 18.6 percent.

## CONCLUSION

In numerous respects, media treatment of the "other" polls of the election campaign had even more shortcomings than media coverage of the Canada-wide polls. Many methodological elements were missing or inaccurate in media reports on the polls (see table 1.17). For some elements, such as initial sample size and sampling methods, much more information was given on the "other" polls than on Canada-wide polls. Nevertheless, in no case did we find complete, systematic reports on the technical elements of published polls, much less a methodological insert.

The special case of the Quebec polls should be noted. Quebec

Table 1.17
**Missing or inaccurate methodological elements in "other" polls published during the 1988 federal election campaign**

| Methodological standards | Reports missing this information | |
|---|---|---|
| | N | % |
| Sponsors | 7 | 19 |
| Period of interviews | 12 | 32 |
| Collection method | 10 | 27 |
| Sampling base | 2 | 5 |
| Sample size | 31 | 84 |
| Number of ineligible people | 33 | 89 |
| Rejection rate | 37 | 100 |
| Sampling method | 28 | 76 |
| Number of respondents | 3 | 8 |
| Response rate | 29 | 78 |
| Margin of error | 11 | 30 |
| Weighting or adjustment factors | 24 | 65 |

journalists generally provide much more detail on the methodological aspects of polls than do those in other parts of the country. Even so, numerous deficiencies still have to be corrected. The situation in Quebec is explained in part by the presence of the polling committee of the Regroupement québécois des sciences sociales. Several times during the 1988 election campaign, the committee advocated adherence to certain methodological standards. In addition, the committee urged individual polling organizations at various points in the campaign to insist that the print and electronic media present methodology when reporting poll results. As we have noted, however, there is still room for improvement.

The regional polls we examined were not particularly good at predicting voting intentions or constituency winners. In general, spreads were well outside margins of error, and ultimately these polls reflected a somewhat distorted picture of reality. Perhaps they did constitute a clear picture of the status of public opinion at the time they were conducted. If this is true, the electorate at a provincial, regional or local level is far more volatile than the Canadian electorate as a whole; but this interpretation is likely excessive. A refinement in techniques is called for.

In the preceding analysis, we have attempted to assess the extent to which journalists and the media have adhered to the methodological standards recommended by the polling committee, standards that are similar to journalistic codes of ethics. In emphasizing departures from the standards, we have raised questions about the technical preparation of polls, mentioning only occasionally how the written press has dealt with all the information in polling reports through graphics and headlines. These aspects of the journalistic treatment of polls no doubt merit further study, but the picture already painted reveals significant shortcomings and problems that must be remedied, as much by journalists and broadcasters as by polling organizations.

The picture may appear darker than it really is. It could be argued that the media treatment of polls is far superior to that in other countries, even where polling commissions exist. The Quebec situation is interesting from this perspective and could no doubt convince the supporters of self-regulation that adherence to ethical standards constitutes the first step toward improving the situation. The polling committee has existed in Quebec since 1977, and some improvement in the presentation of polls in the written press has been seen. But progress over the past 10 years seems limited if one considers how variable the degree of adherence to methodological standards is, even for polls conducted by the same organization. If self-regulation has produced such poor results, what can we conclude?

# 9

# REGULATING OPINION POLLS DURING AND OUTSIDE ELECTION PERIODS
## *Options and Recommendations*

I N LIGHT OF THE OBSERVATIONS and conclusions in this study, certain fundamental questions should guide decisions about the regulation of polls:

1. How can one ensure greater equity between the written press and electronic media within the Canadian legal framework and in the light of possible interpretations of the *Canadian Charter of Rights and Freedoms?*
2. Is imposing a blackout sufficient to allow citizens to exercise their right of rejoinder? If so, how long should this period be?
3. Have polling organizations demonstrated sufficient openness and taken the necessary steps to correct or improve polling practices? Have they made sufficient efforts to comply with the methodological and ethical standards they themselves established?
4. Do the print and electronic media publish or broadcast enough technical information to allow Canadian electors to evaluate the reliability and quality of published polls?
5. How can legislators and those involved in polling and disseminating polling results promote procedures or mechanisms that would allow public access to all technical information related to polls? In other words, how can the right to information and to verifiable information be facilitated?

### A 72-HOUR BLACKOUT FOR THE PRINT AND ELECTRONIC MEDIA

Given that

- legislators should specify whether opinion polls represent partisan information and whether the 48-hour rule applies to polls;
- there is evidently some concern in Canada about special treatment for the print and electronic media with respect to disseminating partisan information, including polls, during an election period;
- any legislation whose objective is to prohibit opinion polls during a certain period must take into consideration its effects on freedom of speech and on the public's right to information; and
- the public must be allowed to exercise its right of rejoinder within a reasonable period,

we make the following recommendations:

1. A 72-hour blackout should be imposed equally on all print and electronic media.
2. Exit polls should be prohibited in Canada; no poll should be made public before the last polling station closes.

### PUBLICATION OF A METHODOLOGY INSERT OR A SURVEY SPECIFICATIONS SHEET

Given that

- there are significant shortcomings in the media treatment of polls;
- journalists and broadcasters do not adhere to their own standards on the publication and broadcasting of certain methodological information;
- legislative measures requiring that certain methodological information accompany the publication or broadcast of opinion polls do not infringe on freedom of speech but rather ensure the public's right to complete and accurate information;
- the public has the right to demand complete and accurate information, both during and outside election periods, for all polls, no matter who the sponsor; and
- *all pre-election polls*, including government ones, should be accompanied by these various elements,

we make the following recommendations:

3. All published or broadcast polls should be accompanied by a survey specifications sheet (an example is shown in table 1.18).
4. A standardized methodology insert, as proposed in this study, should accompany the publication or broadcast of any poll in Canada.
5. Voting intentions should be presented as in table 1.18 and be accompanied by all the information listed there.

### MONITORING POLLS: THE CREATION OF A POLLING COMMISSION

Given that

- in Canada there is no institution with the authority to monitor or regulate polls during and outside election periods;
- polling organizations have not unequivocally demonstrated a desire to improve the contents of their reports;
- there is no organization to guarantee the confidentiality of data on respondents, and no precise mechanism guaranteeing this confidentiality is set out in the reports of the polling institutes;
- not all poll reports made public are easily accessible;
- the only entity that has exercised a supervisory role for the past 10 years (and then only for polls published or broadcast in Quebec), the polling committee of the Regroupement québécois des sciences sociales, has not succeeded in enforcing its methodological standards on the road to self-regulation; and
- there is no similar committee in other provinces or at the federal level (although several researchers have taken on the task on occasion, mainly during election campaigns),

we make the following recommendations:

6. A polling commission should be established, independent of political parties, polling organizations and the media, to ensure that the media publish or broadcast complete methodological information, that polling organizations safeguard the confidentiality of data and not use them for commercial or other purposes, and that the public's right to high-quality information is protected.
7. The law should provide for the prosecution of and fines for anyone who fails to protect the confidentiality of data or to publish a methodology insert.
8. The polling commission should be under the authority of the chief electoral officer, and its composition should be specified by regulation.

**Table 1.18**
**Sample of a methodology insert to accompany the publication or broadcast of all polls**

| Polling methodology* | |
|---|---|
| Polling organization | Tendance Inc. |
| Sponsor | Le Journal |
| Data-collection period | 17–20 August 1991 |
| Data-collection method | Telephone |
| Population | Canada (with right to vote) |
| Initial sample | 1 678 |
| Number ineligible | 200 |
| Percentage screened out | 11.9 |
| Number of respondents | 1 000 |
| Percentage of respondents | 67.7 |
| Margin of error | ±3.16 (19/20 times) |
| Weighting variables | Region, age, sex |
| Sampling method | Stratified |

| Voting intentions | | |
|---|---|---|

Question:

| | Unweighted data | |
|---|---|---|
| | N | % |
| Conservative candidate | 350 | 35 |
| Liberal candidate | 350 | 35 |
| New Democratic candidate | 150 | 15 |
| Other candidates | 40 | 4 |
| Will destroy ballot | 10 | 1 |
| Will not vote | 10 | 1 |
| Did not know | 20 | 2 |
| Refused to respond | 70 | 7 |
| Total | 1 000 | 100 |

*Source:* Chief Electoral Officer of Canada.
*To obtain poll results, contact: person responsible.

9. Polling organizations, the media, governments and candidates should be obliged to deposit with the polling commission all pertinent information on the production of a poll and the dissemination of its results the same day the poll is published or broadcast during an election period.

10. All our recommendations should apply to the periods during which elections and referendums are held.

## OBSERVATIONS AND CONCLUSION

In the light of our recommendations, several questions arise. What are the immediate advantages of implementing these recommendations in Canada? Can they be implemented by broadcasters? What could citizens, interested or not in election campaigns, learn from the application of these measures?

For now, we believe that all the proposed measures constitute a minimum that is neither too lax nor too excessive and will provide a better response to the demands of Canadians and the requirements of a democratic society. The 72-hour blackout suggested here would put print and broadcast journalists on the same footing and would respond to a long-standing grievance among broadcast journalists that they face more restrictions than their print colleagues. The legislator could envisage eliminating the 48-hour rule entirely, but such a route might jeopardize a relative consensus on the need to limit all partisan information at the end of a campaign. A supplementary 24 hours would enable citizens to exercise their moral right to reply, which would encourage public discussion, especially when it is a matter of deciding who will govern us for the next few years. Broadcasters and citizens should, therefore, draw dividends from this measure.

Our first recommendation advocates a ban on the broadcasting of any type of poll, including exit polls, for 72 hours prior to the closing of the last polling station. It is not our intention to ban polling, for each organization should be able to conduct as many surveys as it wishes. None of our recommendations advocates restricting publication of public opinion data after the last polling station in Canada closes. Broadcasters and newspaper editors could release the results of any poll as soon as the last polling station closes, as Canadians would already have made their choice by then. Since only the electronic media are affected by this measure, this would avoid the crazy race that occurs among the U.S. networks to see who will be the first to predict the winner of the election. Our proposal is not designed to limit the efforts of Canadian television networks to make predictions; they will simply have to use methods other than polling techniques. However, this last issue also raises the question of when broadcasters will be able to go on the air in each region. However, that is another debate.

We think that it will also be easy to implement our recommendation that the publication or broadcasting of any poll be accompanied by a specifications sheet or methodology insert containing the most relevant information needed to understand the results of a survey, and in particular, voting intentions. Journalists have often asked for a typical insert that would help them synthesize the essential information. We have, therefore, compiled 13 items that we have found in all the codes formulated by various interveners; according to many people, these are the key items for accurately assessing the quality of a poll. All the items in this grid can easily be presented to radio listeners. For television, we see no major difficulty in transposing this grid to the screen. Broadcasters often do it these days. To relieve the monotony of everyone using the same insert, the media should be able to find innovative ways of presenting the other results. Although uniformity certainly has its drawbacks, the use of this insert will enable everyone to recognize the limitations that exist in the interpretation of each survey and allow them to compare the methodologies. In our experience, identifying these items would help to ensure that every survey is properly conducted, from the drafting of the questionnaire to the publication of results. These are, after all, minimum standards.

As for the final section of our recommendations dealing with the creation of a polling commission, we believe that although its primary role should be monitoring, it should also act as a driving force among researchers, pollsters, broadcasters and citizens. Thus, such a commission could advise both pollsters and broadcasters, inform the public by giving it access to poll data and educate through training sessions, for example, while promoting the need for smoothly functioning democratic rules. This is why we believe that the role could easily be assumed by the office of the chief electoral officer, whose current functions are essentially similar.

Finally, we consider it essential for legislators to enshrine in the *Canada Elections Act* all measures deemed necessary to ensure adherence to methodological and ethical standards in polling, including the individual's right to privacy. We do not propose that these measures be applied outside of election periods. However, we hope that regulating polls during election periods will have a snowball effect on polls in general. We hope that an effective process of self-regulation will emerge, with the polling organizations and the news media monitoring their own behaviour. While experience to date has not been encouraging on this point, a legislative model directed to election polling and concern for the credibility of polling might lead to higher standards.

# NOTES

In this study, quoted material that originated in French has been translated into English.

1. Butler and Kavanagh (1988, 125) state that this number is 73. Robert Worcester (1991, 110), however, mentions 55 national polls. Pippa Norris (1989, 224) estimates this to be 40.

2. This typology has been adapted from that used in the book by Alfred Max (1981, 132–33).

3. We have catalogued more than 1 700 titles covering polling. This range of titles also serves as an indication of the many facets of public opinion and the many definitions that apply to it.

4. It should be noted that this writer makes two errors in analysing the situation: the *Broadcasting Act* was not passed in 1969, as he states, but rather in 1968; and this is not section 116 of the *Broadcasting Act*, but rather section 28.

5. This unreported decision of 29 March 1974 was upheld by the Ontario Court of Appeal (*R. v. CFRB* 1976).

6. See also France, Decree No. 78–79 and Decree No. 80–351.

7. Frizzell has listed 24 Canada-wide surveys conducted during the campaign. However, data from the Gallup poll published in the 10 October edition of the *Toronto Star* were collected only from the Toronto and area population. The Environics poll of 10 November was the second stage of a poll; the first occurred between 25 and 26 October and the second between 28 and 30 October; we chose to separate these two events. Finally, we excluded the Goldfarb survey of 2 November, as it was obviously a leaked poll with very compartmentalized results (Frizzell 1989, 95).

8. Our figures differ in several cases from those presented by Frizzell, and we have no explanation for these differences. We drew from all the results before the undecideds were redistributed in the reports from the polling organizations, when the reports were available, and compared these results with those published in the newspapers.

9. Vincent Lemieux uses "échantillon de départ" (initial sample) for what we would call "échantillon final" (final sample); he uses "échantillon d'arrivée" (end sample) when referring to the number of respondents who completed the survey. We prefer to use "nombre de répondants" (number of respondents), because it is no longer a question of sample, strictly speaking: several people refused to answer the questionnaire for various reasons.

10. We have included these polls in the analysis, although an evaluation of their televised presentation would probably be necessary to judge their journalistic treatment.

11. Even in the case of polls funded by the Social Sciences and Humanities Research Council of Canada, the research team awarded the grant to conduct the federal election study of 1988 – professors André Blais (Université de Montréal), Richard Johnston (the University of British Columbia), Henry E. Brady (University of California, Berkeley) and Jean Crête (Université Laval) – subcontracted the fieldwork to a Toronto institution, York University.

# BIBLIOGRAPHY

## ABBREVIATIONS

| | |
|---|---|
| A.P.R. | Alberta Provincial Reports |
| Alta L.R. (2d) | Alberta Law Reports (Second Series) |
| am. | amended |
| c. | chapter |
| C.A. | Court of Appeal |
| C.C.C. | Criminal Court Cases |
| Div. Ct. | Divisional Court |
| D.L.R. | Dominion Law Reports |
| F.C.A. | Federal Court of Appeal |
| H.C. | High Court |
| J.O. | Journal officiel (France) |
| Nfld. & P.E.I.R. | Newfoundland and Prince Edward Island Reports |
| Nfld. Prov. Ct. | Newfoundland Provincial Court |
| O.R. | Ontario Reports |
| Q.B. | Queen's Bench |
| R.S.A. | Revised Statutes of Alberta |
| R.S.B.C. | Revised Statutes of British Columbia |
| R.S.C. | Revised Statutes of Canada |
| R.S.N.B. | Revised Statutes of New Brunswick |
| R.S.N.S. | Revised Statutes of Nova Scotia |
| S.B.C. | Statutes of British Columbia |
| S.C. | Statutes of Canada |
| s(s). | section(s) |
| Supp. | Supplement |
| U.K. | United Kingdom |
| U.S. | United States Supreme Court Reports |

AAPOR. 1948–49. "Standards in Public Opinion Research." *Public Opinion Quarterly* 12:812–15.

Adams, Michael, et al. 1988a. "1515 Eligible Voters Were Interviewed for Poll." *Globe and Mail*, 12 October, A10.

———. 1988b. "Liberals Move Ahead of PCs in Wake of Leaders' Debates." *Globe and Mail*, 1 November, A12.

Alberta. *Elections Act*, R.S.A. 1980, c. E-2.

Antoine, Jacques. 1985. "L'industrie des sondages." *Projet* 193:90–102.

———. 1987. "Les Sondages d'opinion: où en est-on?" *Revue française de marketing* 112:78–81.

———. 1989. "Le Point sur les sondages d'opinion." *Revue française de marketing* 123:29–32.

Association canadienne de la radio et de la télévision de langue française (ACRTF). 1990. Brief presented to the Royal Commission on Electoral Reform and Party Financing. Ottawa.

Association de l'industrie de la recherche marketing et sociale. 1991. *Goals and Standards.* Montreal: AIRMS.

Beaud, Jean-Pierre. 1989. "Les Sondages et les élections: le cas de la campagne électorale fédérale de 1988." Montreal: Université du Québec à Montréal.

Beckton, Clare. 1989. "Freedom of Expression (Section 2(b))." In *The Canadian Charter of Rights and Freedoms.* 2d ed., ed. Gérald-A. Beaudoin and Ed Ratushny. Toronto: Carswell.

Beed, Terence W. 1977. "Opinion Polling and the Elections." In *Australia at the Polls – The National Election of 1975,* ed. Howard R. Penniman. Washington, DC: American Enterprise Institute for Public Policy Research.

Belgium. 1985. *Loi relative à la publication des sondages d'opinion.* 18 July.

Black, Peter. 1988. "Grits Soar in Latest Poll." *Montreal Daily News,* 31 October, 7.

Blais, André, Richard Johnston, Henry E. Brady and Jean Crête. 1990. "The Dynamics of Horse Race Expectations in the 1988 Canadian Election." Paper presented at the convention of the Canadian Political Science Association, 27–29 May.

Board of Broadcast Governors. 1961. *White Paper on Political and Controversial Broadcasting Policies.* Ottawa: BBG.

Bogart, Leo. 1985. *Polls and the Awareness of Public Opinion.* New Brunswick: Transaction Books.

Boursin, Jean-Louis. 1990. *Les Dés et les urnes – les calculs de la démocratie.* Paris: Seuil.

British Columbia. *Election Act,* R.S.B.C. 1979, c. 103.

———. *Election Amendment Act,* S.B.C. 1982, c. 148.

British Press Council. 1977. "Insidious Interference with the Freedom of the Press – 21 August 1967." *Sondages* 39:163–64.

Butler, David, and Dennis Kavanagh. 1984. *The British General Election of 1983.* London: Macmillan.

———. 1988. *The British General Election of 1987.* New York: St. Martin's.

Butler, David, and Richard Rose. 1960. *The British General Election of 1959.* London: Macmillan.

Calmes, Jacqueline. 1984. "Exit Polls Targeted – Method Sought to Restrict Broadcast Vote Predictions." *Congressional Quarterly* (10 March): 565–66.

Canada. *An Act to amend the Election Act*, Bill C-79.

———. *Broadcasting Act*, S.C. 1967–68, c. 25.

———. *Broadcasting Act*, R.S.C. 1970, c. B-11, am. 1973–74, c. 51.

———. *Broadcasting Act*, S.C. 1991, c. 11.

———. *Canada Elections Act*, R.S.C. 1970, c. 14 (1st Supp.).

———. *Canada Elections Act*, R.S.C. 1985, c. E-2.

———. *Canadian Bill of Rights*, R.S.C. 1985, Appendix II.

———. *Canadian Charter of Rights and Freedoms*, ss. 1, 2. Part I of the *Constitution Act, 1982*, being Schedule B of the *Canada Act 1982* (U.K.), 1982, c. 11.

Canada. Chief Electoral Officer. 1989. *Report of the Chief Electoral Officer of Canada as per subsection 195(1) of the Canada Elections Act*. Ottawa: Minister of Supply and Services Canada.

Canada. Committee on Election Expenses. 1966. *Report*. Ottawa: Queen's Printer.

Canada. Consultative Group on Survey Research. 1976. *Survey Research: Report*. Ottawa: Minister of Supply and Services Canada.

Canada. House of Commons. Standing Committee on Privileges and Elections. 1976. *Minutes of Proceedings and Evidence*. Ottawa: Queen's Printer.

Canadian Advertising Research Foundation. 1984. *Recherche en publicité – normes et méthodes*. CARF.

Canadian Association of Broadcasters. 1990. Brief presented to the Royal Commission on Electoral Reform and Party Financing. Ottawa.

Canadian Broadcasting Corporation (CBC). 1975. *Les Sondages d'opinion politique et leur utilisation par les mass media*. Ottawa.

———. 1988. *Élections fédérales 1988 – sondage de Radio-Canada*. 16 October. Ottawa.

———. 1990. Brief presented to the Royal Commission on Electoral Reform and Party Financing. Ottawa.

Canadian Daily Newspaper Publishers Association. 1980. *La Couverture des sondages: quelques conseils pratiques*. Toronto.

Canadian National Election Study. 1988. Institute for Social Research, York University. Principal investigators: Richard Johnston, André Blais, Henry E. Brady and Jean Crête. Funded by the Social Sciences and Humanities Research Council.

Canadian Radio-Television Commission (CRTC). 1968. *CRTC Announcement: Broadcasters as Political Candidates*. Ottawa: CRTC.

Cantril, Albert H. 1991. *The Opinion Connection: Polling, Politics and the Press*. Washington, DC: Congressional Quarterly Press.

Ceci, Stephen J., and Edward L. Kain. 1982. "Jumping on the Bandwagon with the Underdog: The Impact of Attitude Polls on Polling Behavior." *Public Opinion Quarterly* 46:228–42.

*CFRB Ltd. v. Canada (Attorney General) (No. 1)*, [1973] 1 O.R. 57 (Div. Ct.).

*CFRB Ltd. v. Canada (Attorney General) (No. 2)*, [1973] 1 O.R. 79 (H.C.).

*CFRB Ltd. v. Canada (Attorney General)*, [1973] 3 O.R. 819 (C.A.).

Clarke, Harold D., Lawrence LeDuc, Jane Jenson and Jon H. Pammett. 1991. *Absent Mandate – Interpreting Change in Canadian Elections.* 2d ed. Toronto: Gage.

Cloutier, Édouard. 1982. "Les Sondages en tant qu'objets de pouvoirs: le cas de la législation générale dans certains pays occidentaux." Paper presented at the annual meeting of the Canadian Political Science Association, 9 June.

Cloutier, Édouard, Richard Nadeau and Jean Guay. 1989. "Bandwagoning and Underdogging on North American Free Trade: A Quasi-Experimental Panel Study of Opinion Movement." *International Journal of Public Opinion Research* 1:206–20.

Comité des sondages. 1979. *Sondages politiques et politique des sondages au Québec.* Montreal: Société québécoise de science politique and Université du Québec à Montréal.

Commission des droits de la personne du Québec. 1979. *Commentaires sur la question de la réglementation des enquêtes par sondage d'opinion en période électorale ou référendaire.* Document adopted by the Commission, Resolution COM-80-8.3. 6 April.

Conseil de presse du Québec. 1980. "Les Sondages et le droit à l'information." *Le Devoir*, 8 February, 2, 4.

Council of Europe. 1985. *Assemblée parlementaire: rapport d'information sur les sondages d'opinion présenté par la Commission des relations avec les parlementaires nationaux et le public.* Document 5449, 29 August.

Crespi, Irving. 1989. *Public Opinion Polls and Democracy.* Boulder: Westview Press.

Crouzet, Philippe. 1985. "La Jurisprudence de la Commission des sondages." *Pouvoirs* 33:57–77.

Delisle, Norman. 1990. "125 stations privées de radio et de télévision créeront leur propre tribunal de déontologie." *Le Devoir*, 6 November, A3.

Delli Carpini, Michael. 1984. "Scooping the Voters? The Consequences of the Networks' Early Call of the 1980 Presidential Race." *Journal of Politics* 46:866–85.

Dubois, Philip L. 1983. "Election Night Projections and Voter Turnout in the West: A Note on the Hazards of Aggregate Data Analysis." *American Politics Quarterly* 11:349–63.

Duff, Jim. 1988. "Island Is Lib Solid, but Mostly Tory Outside." *Montreal Daily News*, 14 November, 2.

Forgues, André. 1988. "Le PC reste premier au Québec." *Le Soleil*, 18 November, A1.

France. *Décret n° 78–79*, J.O., 26 janvier 1978, p. 503.

———. *Décret n° 80–351*, J.O., 17 mai 1980, p. 1226.

———. *Loi du 19 juillet 1977*, J.O., 20 juillet 1977, p. 3837.

Frizzell, Alan. 1989. "The Perils of Polling." In *The Canadian General Election of 1988*, ed. Alan Frizzell et al. Ottawa: Carleton University Press.

Frizzell, Alan, and Anthony Westell. 1985. *The Canadian General Election of 1984*. Ottawa: Carleton University Press.

Fuchs, Douglas A. 1966. "Election-Day Radio-Television and Western Voting." *Public Opinion Quarterly* 30:226–37.

Gallup, George. 1944. *A Guide to Public Opinion Polls*. Princeton: Princeton University Press.

———. 1972. *The Sophisticated Poll Watcher's Guide*. Princeton: Princeton University Press.

*Gazette* (Montreal). 1988. "Poll in Quebec Gives Tories 44% and Liberals 36%." 18 November, A1.

Gazier, François. 1989. "Bilan de la Commission des sondages." *Journal de la Société de statistique de Paris* 130 (4): 201–205.

Gazier, François, and Jean-Frédéric de Leusse. 1988. "La Commission des sondages face à l'élection présidentielle de 1988." Paris: Commission des sondages.

Germany. *Basic Law for the Federal Republic of Germany* [Constitution], 1949.

———. 1986. *Electoral Law*. Cologne: Nettsheim Druck GmbH.

Gerstlé, Jacques. 1991. "Election Communication in France." In *Media, Elections and Democracy*, ed. Frederick J. Fletcher. Vol. 19 of the research studies of the Royal Commission on Electoral Reform and Party Financing. Ottawa and Toronto: RCERPF/Dundurn.

*Globe and Mail*. 1988. "Changes in Voting Tracked." 10 November.

Greenshields, Vern. 1988a. "Poll Indicates Tight Race in Two Saskatoon Ridings." *Star Phoenix*, 10 November, A1.

———. 1988b. "Saskatoon Voters Key on Free Trade in Election: Poll." *Star Phoenix*, 10 November, A3.

Herman, Valentine, and Francine Mendel. 1977. *Les Parlements dans le monde: recueil de données comparatives*. Paris: PUF for Union interparlementaire.

Hoy, Claire. 1989. *Margin of Error – Pollsters and the Manipulation of Canadian Politics*. Toronto: Key Porter Books.

*Institut international de statistique.* 1926. Vol. 22, part 1. Rome.

Jackson, John E. 1983. "Election Night Reporting and Voter Turnout." *American Journal of Political Science* 27:613–35.

Javeau, Camille, and Catherine Vigneron. 1989. *Les Secrets des sondages enfin révélés.* Brussels: Éditions Labor.

Jessen, Raymond J., Richard H. Blythe, Jr., Oscar Kempthorne and W. Edwards Deming. 1947. "On a Population Sample for Greece." *Journal of the American Statistical Association* 42:357–84.

Johnson, David B. 1991. *Public Choice – An Introduction to the New Political Economy.* Mountain View: Bristlecone Books.

Kay, Barry J. 1990. "Improving upon the Cube Law: A Regional Swing Model for Converting Canadian Popular Votes into Parliamentary Seats." Paper presented at the annual meeting of the Canadian Political Science Association, 27 May.

Kennedy, Mark. 1988. "Liberals Lead in PC Polls, PM Admits." *Gazette* (Montreal), 8 November, A11.

Kushner, Howard. 1983. "Election Polls, Freedom of Speech and the Constitution." *Ottawa Law Review* 15:515–52.

Lachapelle, Guy. 1986. "Les Répondants-discrets et l'élection québécoise de 1985." *Politique* 10:31–54.

Lachapelle, Guy, Édouard Cloutier and Jean-Pierre Beaud. 1989. "Sonder, oui, mais il faut aussi bien informer le public." *La Presse,* 20 September, B3.

Lakeman, Énid. 1974. *How Democracies Vote.* London: Faber and Faber.

Lavoie, Gilbert. 1988. "Le PC conteste Gallup." *La Presse,* 9 November, B5.

Lazareff, Alexandre. 1984. *Le Droit des sondages politiques: analyse de la réglementation française.* Paris: Librairie générale de droit et de jurisprudence.

*Le Devoir.* 1988. "La Région de Québec votera en bloc pour les conservateurs." 19 November, 1.

Lemieux, Louise. 1988. "Le Dernier sondage IQOP accorde une avance de 35% aux conservateurs." *Le Soleil,* 19 November, A9.

Lemieux, Vincent. 1988. *Les Sondages et la démocratie.* Quebec: Institut québécois de recherche sur la culture.

Ley, F.L. 1976. *Commonwealth Electoral Procedures.* Canberra: Australian Government Publishing Service.

Magnant, Michel. 1980. *Les Sondages d'opinion.* Ottawa: Parliamentary Library, Bulletin 80-22F, 28 November.

*Mahoney v. Newfoundland Broadcasting Co. Ltd.; R. v. Newfoundland Broadcasting Co. Ltd.* (1981), 30 Nfld. & P.E.I.R. 68, 84 A.P.R. 68 (Nfld. Prov. Ct.).

Mahoney, Kathleen, and Sheilah L. Martin. 1985. *Broadcasting and the Canadian Charter of Human Rights and Freedoms: Justifications for Restricting Freedom of Expression*. Report prepared for the Task Force on Broadcasting Policy. Ottawa.

Marsh, Catherine. 1984. "Back on the Bandwagon: The Effect of Opinion Polls on Public Opinion." *British Journal of Political Science* 15:51–74.

Max, Alfred. 1981. *La République des sondages*. Paris: Gallimard.

McFarland, Janet. 1988. "Poll Angers Tories – Huge Margin of Error Cited in Survey." *Winnipeg Free Press*, 3 November, 1, 4.

Meisel, John. 1985. "The Decline of Party in Canada." In *Party Politics in Canada*. 5th ed., ed. Hugh G. Thorburn. Scarborough: Prentice-Hall Canada.

Mendelsohn, Harold. 1966. "Election-Day Broadcasts and Terminal Voting Decisions." *Public Opinion Quarterly* 30:212–25.

Mendelsohn, Harold, and Irving Crespi. 1970. *Polls, Television and the New Politics*. Scranton: Chandler Publishing.

Meynaud, Hélène, and Denis Duclos. 1985. *Les Sondages d'opinion*. Paris: Éditions La Découverte.

Milavsky, J. Ronald, et al. 1985. "Early Calls of Election Results and Exit Polls: Pros, Cons and Constitutional Considerations." *Public Opinion Quarterly* 49:1–18.

*Mills v. Alabama*, 384 U.S. 214 (1966).

Mitofsky, Warren J. 1991. "A Short History of Exit Polls." In *Polling and Presidential Election Coverage*, ed. Paul J. Lavrakas and Jack K. Holley. Newbury Park: Sage Publications.

*Montreal Daily News*. 1988. "The Poll: 827 Surveyed in Greater Montreal Area." 14 November, 3.

Mosteller, Frederick, et al. 1949. *The Pre-election Polls of 1948 – Report of Committee on Analysis of Pre-election Polls and Forecasts*. Bulletin 60. New York: Social Science Research Council.

*National Citizens' Coalition Inc. v. Canada (Attorney General)* (1984), 32 Alta L.R. (2d) 249 (Q.B.).

New Brunswick. *Elections Act*, R.S.N.B. 1973, c. E-3.

New York. *Fair Campaign Code*, Part 6201 of *The Election Law*, 1976, c. 233.

New York. State Board of Elections. 1990. "1984 Opinion of the State Board of Elections #1." In *Formal Opinions – 1984*. Albany: State of New York.

Nocera, Joseph. 1984. "Providence Diarist: The Perils of Polling." *New Republic* 190 (9 April): 42.

Noelle-Neumann, Élisabeth. 1984. *The Spiral of Silence – Public Opinion, Our Social Skin*. Chicago: University of Chicago Press.

Norris, Pippa. 1989. "The Emergence of Polls of Marginals in the 1987 Election: Their Role and Record." In *Political Communications – The General Election Campaign of 1987*, ed. Ivor Crewe and Martin Harrop. New York: Cambridge University Press.

Nova Scotia. *Election Act*, R.S.N.S. 1967, c. 83.

Ontario. 1978. *Debates*, 27–28 April.

Ontario. 1979. *Debates*, May.

*Ottawa Citizen*. 1988. "Tories Bounce Back, Poll Shows." 10 November, A1.

Perry, Roland. 1984. *Hidden Power – The Programming of the President*. New York: Beaufort Books.

Porado, Philip. 1990. "Will the Exit Poll Work?" *Campaigns & Elections* 11:46–48.

Qualter, Terence. 1968. "Seats and Votes: An Application of the Cube Law to the Canadian Electoral System." *Canadian Journal of Political Science* 1:336–44.

Quebec. 1979–80. *Journal des débats*, 31st Legislature, 4th session.

———. 1983–84. *Journal des débats*, 32nd Legislature, 4th session.

———. 1984–85. *Journal des débats*, 32nd Legislature, 5th session.

*R. v. CFRB Ltd.* (1976), 30 C.C.C. (2d) 386 (Ont C.A.).

*Reference re Regulation and Control of Radio Communication*, [1932] 2 D.L.R. 81.

*Reference re New Brunswick Broadcasting Co. Ltd. and the CRTC* (1985), 13 D.L.R. (4th) 77 (F.C.A.).

Robinson, Claude E. 1932. *Straw Votes*. New York: Columbia University Press.

Sadouin, Roland. 1973. "Pour une discipline des sondages." *La Nef* (December).

Sanders, Wilfrid. 1943. *Jack and Jacques: A Scientific Approach to the Study of French and Non-French Taught in Canada*. Toronto: Ryerson Press.

Solinge, Jacques van. 1988. "Haro sur les sondages." *Le Soir*, 29 September.

Soderlund, Walter C., Walter I. Romanow, E. Donald Briggs and Ronald H. Wagenberg. 1984. *Media and Elections in Canada*. Toronto: Holt, Rinehart and Winston of Canada.

*Sondages*. 1977. "Recommendations de la conférence du Speaker de la Chambre des communes relatives à la publication des sondages en période électorale, et réponse du gouvernement." 39:161.

Sormany, Pierre. 1990. *Le métier de journaliste: guide des outils et des pratiques du journalisme au Québec*. Montreal: Boréal.

Spafford, Duff. 1970. "The Electoral System of Canada." *American Political Science Review* 64:168–76.

Stoetzel, Jean. 1980. "Les Sondages d'opinion: aspects déontologiques." *Encyclopedia Universalis.*

Stoetzel, Jean, and Alain Girard. 1973. *Les Sondages d'opinion publique.* Paris: PUF.

Sudman, Seymour. 1986. "Do Exit Polls Influence Voting Behavior?" *Public Opinion Quarterly* 50:331–39.

*Toronto Star.* 1988. "Tories Top Poll at 43%, Trade Seen as Key Issue." 3 October, A1.

Tremblay, Victor. 1986. "Critères pratiques pour la définition des classes de pondération." *Techniques d'enquêtes* 12 (1): 91–103.

Wald, Kenneth D. 1985. "The Closeness Turnout Hypothesis: A Reconsideration." *American Politics Quarterly* 13:273–96.

Waller, Robert. 1987. "The ITN-Harris Exit Poll 1987." *Journal of the Market Research Society* 29:419–28.

———. 1989. "Constituency Polling in the 1987 Election." In *Political Communications – The General Election Campaign of 1987,* ed. Ivor Crewe and Martin Harrop. New York: Cambridge University Press.

WAPOR. 1983. "Code of Professional Ethics and Practices." In *Political Opinion Polling – An International Review,* ed. Robert M. Worcester. New York: St. Martin's Press.

Whalen, Hugh. 1970. "The Perils of Polling." In *Politics: Canada – Culture and Process.* 3d ed., ed. Paul Fox. Toronto: McGraw-Hill.

Worcester, Robert M. 1984. *Proposals for Regulating or Banning the Taking or Publication of Opinion Polls.* Paper presented to the WAPOR conference, Wisconsin, 17 May.

———. 1991. *British Public Opinion: A Guide to the History and Methodology of Political Opinion Polling.* London: Basil Blackwell.

# Acknowledgements

The Royal Commission on Electoral Reform and Party Financing and the publishers wish to acknowledge with gratitude the permission of the following to reprint and translate material:

Association de l'industrie de la recherche marketing et sociale; Basil Blackwell; Cambridge University Press; Canada Council; *The Globe and Mail*; Howard Kushner; Minister of Supply and Services Canada; Toronto Star Syndicate; Robert M. Worcester.

Care has been taken to trace the ownership of copyright material used in the text, including the tables and figures. The authors and publishers welcome any information enabling them to rectify any reference or credit in subsequent editions.

~

Consistent with the Commission's objective of promoting full participation in the electoral system by all segments of Canadian society, gender neutrality has been used wherever possible in the editing of the research studies.

# THE COLLECTED RESEARCH STUDIES*

* The titles of studies may not be final in all cases.

# COMMISSION ORGANIZATION

**CHAIRMAN**
Pierre Lortie

**COMMISSIONERS**
Pierre Fortier
Robert Gabor
William Knight
Lucie Pépin

**SENIOR OFFICERS**

*Executive Director*
Guy Goulard

*Director of Research*
Peter Aucoin

*Special Adviser to the Chairman*
Jean-Marc Hamel

*Research*
F. Leslie Seidle,
    Senior Research Coordinator

*Legislation*
Jules Brière, Senior Adviser
Gérard Bertrand
Patrick Orr

*Coordinators*
Herman Bakvis
Michael Cassidy
Frederick J. Fletcher
Janet Hiebert
Kathy Megyery
Robert A. Milen
David Small

*Communications and Publishing*
Richard Rochefort, Director
Hélène Papineau, Assistant
    Director
Paul Morisset, Editor
Kathryn Randle, Editor

*Assistant Coordinators*
David Mac Donald
Cheryl D. Mitchell

*Finance and Administration*
Maurice R. Lacasse, Director

*Contracts and Personnel*
Thérèse Lacasse, Chief

# Editorial, Design and Production Services

## Royal Commission on Electoral Reform and Party Financing

*Editors* Denis Bastien, Susan Becker Davidson, Ginette Bertrand, Louis Bilodeau, Claude Brabant, Louis Chabot, Danielle Chaput, Norman Dahl, Carlos del Burgo, Julie Desgagners, Chantal Granger, Volker Junginger, Denis Landry, André LaRose, Paul Morisset, Christine O'Meara, Mario Pelletier, Marie-Noël Pichelin, Kathryn Randle, Georges Royer, Eve Valiquette, Dominique Vincent.


## Le Centre de Documentation Juridique du Québec Inc.

Hubert Reid, *President*

Claire Grégoire, *Comptroller*

Lucie Poirier, *Production Manager*
Gisèle Gingras, *Special Project Assistant*

*Translators* Pierre-Yves de la Garde, Richard Lapointe, Marie-Josée Turcotte.

*Technical Editors* Stéphane Côté Coulombe, *Coordinator*; Josée Chabot, Danielle Morin.

*Copy Editors* Martine Germain, Lise Larochelle, Élizabeth Reid, Carole St-Louis, Isabelle Tousignant, Charles Tremblay, Sébastien Viau.

*Word Processing* André Vallée.

*Formatting* Typoform, Claude Audet; Linda Goudreau, *Formatting Coordinator*.


## Wilson & Lafleur Ltée

Claude Wilson, *President*

**DUNDURN PRESS**

J. Kirk Howard, *President*
Ian Low, *Comptroller*
Jeanne MacDonald, *Project Coordinator*

Avivah Wargon, *Managing and Production Editor*
Beth Ediger, *Managing Editor*
John St. James, *Managing Editor*
Karen Heese, *Special Project Assistant*

Ruth Chernia, *Tables Editor*
Victoria Grant, *Legal Editor*
Michèle Breton, *Special Editorial Assistant*

*Editorial Staff*   Elliott Chapin, Peggy Foy, Lily Hobel, Marilyn Hryciuk, Madeline Koch, Elizabeth Mitchell, John Shoesmith, Nadine Stoikoff, Shawn Syms, Anne Vespry.

*Copy Editors*   Carol Anderson, Elizabeth d'Anjou, Jane Becker, Diane Brassolotto, Elizabeth Driver, Curtis Fahey, Tony Fairfield, Freya Godard, Frances Hanna, Kathleen Harris, Andria Hourwich, Greg Ioannou, Carlotta Lemieux, Elsha Leventis, David McCorquodale, Virginia Smith, Gail Thorson, Louise Wood.

*Formatting*   Green Graphics; Joanne Green, *Formatting Coordinator*; *Formatters*   Linda Carroll, Mary Ann Cattral, Gail Nina, Eva Payne, Jacqueline Hope Raynor, Ron Rochon, Andy Tong, Carla Vonn Worden, Laura Wilkins.

Printed and bound in Canada by
Best Gagné Book Manufacturers